Speaking & Listening Activities

Hilary Mason & Stephanie Mudd

**Bright Ideas
FOR Early Years**

25p

Published by Scholastic Publications Ltd,
Villiers House, Clarendon Avenue,
Leamington Spa, Warwickshire CV32 5PR

© 1993 Scholastic Publications Ltd

Text © 1993 Hilary Mason and
Stephanie Mudd
Edited by Magdalena Hernas
Illustrations by Jane Bottomley
Photographs by Chris Kelly (pages 5, 7,
19, 29 and 53), Mike Turner (page 37),
Valerie Bissland (page 45), John
Twinning (page 63), David Johnson
(page 71) and Bob Bray (page 79)
Cover design by Joy White
Cover photograph by Martyn Chillmaid

Artwork by Castle Graphics, Kenilworth
Typeset by Typesetters (Birmingham) Ltd
Printed in Great Britain by
The Alden Press Ltd, Oxford

British Library Cataloguing in Publication Data
A catalogue record for this book is available from the
British Library.

ISBN 0 590 53086-0

Contents

Introduction

The importance of speaking and listening in the early years cannot be overemphasised. It is through spoken language that children learn to make sense of their world and to communicate with others. They need to be able to name, describe, interpret and make connections between things that are going on around them all the time, things that we as adults can easily take for granted.

Speaking and listening go hand in hand. Learning how to become a competent talker has to involve active listening, so that children can arrive at an understanding of other people's feelings, thoughts and ideas.

You will find that sometimes most of the speaking and listening happens during the stimulus stage of an activity, in which you introduce children to the ideas you want to get across, and ask for their suggestions and contributions. At other times, talk is used to develop what the children are actually doing during the activity. Other activities draw out the talk that might arise afterwards, to give the children a chance to evaluate their own work and to offer suggestions to others. Some of the activities can be first introduced to the children as a group, to familiarise them with the kinds of talk you want to concentrate on: conversations, recalling incidents, story-telling or getting into other people's shoes, for example. As the children become more familiar with a task, they can explore these forms of talk more independently.

You know your children best, of course, and it may not be appropriate to use all aspects of an activity with every member of your group. This will depend on their age, individual needs and conceptual development. You should, however, find plenty of material to stimulate and satisfy all the children in the class, remembering that the emphasis is on speaking and listening, rather than the finished product.

A book on speaking and listening is incomplete without mentioning the work of the National Oracy Project. The project produces an excellent publication called *Talk*, which is available free of charge from The National Oracy Project, Albion Wharf, 25 Skeldergate, York, YO1 2XI.

Carpet times

Chapter one

However you choose to arrange your activity or teaching groups, there are times when you will want to gather all the children together in one place, to give them a sense of belonging to a larger unit. In early years rooms, this meeting place is often a carpeted area. These are ideal opportunities for speaking and listening activities such as sharing stories and rhymes, playing games and exchanging ideas with the children.

Young children need to learn how to take turns in their talking. It is a good idea to introduce a device such as the 'special talking chairs,' 'magic microphone' or the 'talking stick' which acts as a visual reminder that they have to listen while somebody else is talking.

Say it like this

Focus
Tone and inflection; using voices to reflect emotions and moods.

What you need
A well-known nursery rhyme, verse or refrain such as:

Mix a pancake,
Stir a pancake,
Pop it in the pan.
Fry a pancake,
Toss a pancake,
Catch it if you can.

What to do
Say the rhyme together until the children know it by heart. Take the first line and demonstrate to the children that it can be said in all sorts of ways. Say it in a happy voice, a sad voice, a kind voice and an angry voice. Invite the children to join in. Can they suggest other voices to use?

Then tell the children that one of them will say the rhyme in either a happy or a sad voice while the rest of the group have to guess which one it is. Choose a child to say the rhyme.

Encourage the children to have fun with the rhyme, experimenting with different types of voices: frightened, pleading, old, brave, giggly and so on.

Follow-up
Can the children still guess which voice is being used if they have no clues from facial expression or body language? Try this by asking a child to say the rhyme with their back to the rest of the group.

Good morning – bonjour!

Focus
Encouraging awareness of, and respecting, different ways we use our voices.

What you need
A register of the children's names.

What to do
Tell the children that instead of saying 'Yes, Mr Bartrum' (or whatever your particular convention usually is) when you call their name for the register, today you would like them to answer in a different way, for example, 'Here I am', 'Hello', or 'Good morning'.

When the children have had some practice, draw on their experience of different languages to come up with various ways of greeting each other. Perhaps some of them will have visited other countries or heard various greetings on the television, the radio or in stories. Some children may speak languages other than English at home.

Identify these languages – Arabic, Gujarati, Spanish and so on. Encourage those who speak them to teach the other children some greetings to use when answering the register. Some examples might be the French *'Bonjour Sally'*, to which the reply would be *'Bonjour Monsieur'*; the Muslim greeting *'A salaam alaikum'* and the reply *'Alaikum asaalam'*; or the Spanish *'Buenos días'*.

Follow-up
Organise a theme week and encourage the children to answer the register in an appropriate voice. Try story-book characters (Cinderella, the wolf in Little Red Riding Hood), animals (mouse, bird, lion), fantasy (dragon, alien); or ask the children to invent their own gobbledegook responses.

Spot the deliberate mistake

Focus
Listening carefully and having fun with words.

What you need
A favourite story.

What to do
Choose one of the children's favourite stories. It must be one they know very well. Tell the children they must listen very carefully while you tell the story again, because they will have to spot the deliberate mistakes you are going to make. Ask them to signal (raise their hand) every time they hear a mistake.

Make enough 'errors' to capture their involvement and concentration, but do not go for the overkill or they will get lost!

As you retell the story, make the mistakes very obvious at first. Change the name of the main character, for instance, Henry, rather than Jack, climbed the beanstalk; or change one of the words associated with the story, for example, 'fee, fie, fo, fum' to 'fee, fie, fo, crash'.

Experiment with words or phrases that may alter the meaning, for example, the three little pigs built a ship. This will give the children the idea that the example is ridiculous because a ship does not fit in with the context of the story and is therefore not a reasonable substitute for a house.

Children wil have to listen very carefully indeed if you choose a substitute word that sounds similar, as in 'horse' for 'house'.

Hands can . . .

Focus
Creating poetry together and valuing everbody's contribution.

What you need
A flip-chart or a chalkboard.

Preparation
Before you write you class poem, discuss with the children what they have done with their hands this morning: ate breakfast, got dressed, brushed their teeth, stroked the dog and so on. Extend the talk by encouraging the children to describe other things we can do with our hands: digging the garden, steering vehicles, knitting, painting. You could write down words such as hold, pull, push, squeeze on the flip-chart or board.

What to do
Tell the children they are going to make up a poem about hands. Ask every child to contribute one line. Each line starts with the words 'Hands can'. The lines can be completed with either a single word or a phrase, for example, 'Hands can clap', 'Hands can post a letter.' To help the children with their words and phrases ask them to think back to some of the hand words you identified earlier.

Write their contributions on the flip-chart as the children say them, so you can build them up into a class poem to read together or display.

Follow-up
• The children could use the words you have identified during the initial brainstorm to make up individual 'Hands can' poems.
• Use the same technique to create class poems about other themes such as food, toys, colours or feelings.

Change the lyrics

Focus
Using the rhythms of songs and rhymes as poetry starters.

What you need
Rhymes or songs the children know well. Use ones which have a simple structure and fairly obvious rhythms such as 'Wheels on the bus' and 'Old McDonald's farm'.

Preparation
Whichever song or rhyme you have chosen, make sure the children have the rhythm and words firmly fixed in their minds.

> The wheels on the bus
> Go round and round,
> Round and round,
> Round and round.
> The wheels on the bus
> Go round and round,
> All day long.

What to do
Tell the children they are going to change the song a little. Discuss each of the things mentioned: the wheels, the horn, the wipers. Can they suggest alternative movements, actions and sounds? The horn could go 'honk, honk, honk' instead of 'beep, beep, beep'; the wipers on the bus could go 'slosh, slosh, slosh'. Talk about whether the substitutes still stay true to the rhythm of the original version. Sing it together with the new words to check.

Follow-up
Consider other parts of the bus or people that could make sounds and movements: seats could go 'squeak, squeak, squeak', the radio 'rap, rap, rap,' or the brakes 'sshh, sshh, sshh'.

Tales to tell

Focus
Story-telling in a group.

What you need
Simple hand puppets or a flannel board.

What to do
Ask the children to help you make up a story. It helps to have a stimulus such as simple hand- or finger puppets, or a flannel board to which you can add characters as the story builds up.

Start the story off yourself with, for example, 'Once there was a bear . . .' As you develop the story-line, invite contributions from the children by asking questions such as 'What shall we call the bear?', 'Who do you think he met in the sunny meadow?' All the children should have a chance to contribute, even if they only give you a single word or two.

In order to prevent the children from calling out all at once, and to make them listen carefully to other people's suggestions, establish a way of attracting attention: hands up, sitting in a special 'talking chair' or holding a 'talking stick'.

Follow-up
As the children become more confident with this story-telling technique, let them take more control of the story. They could take turns going round in a circle, offering their own sentences, ideas and cliffhangers.

Listening detectives

Focus
Listening with a purpose.

What you need
A story tape and a tape recorder. There are plenty of commercially produced tapes that work well, for instance, Eric Hill's Spot stories or Mairi Hedderwick's Katie Morag tales. Alternatively, you could record your own story.

What to do
Play a tape of a story the children know well. Tell them that this time they are going to be detectives listening out for something special.

To start with, you could ask the children to listen for a refrain and join in with it: 'Mirror, mirror on the wall', 'Who's been eating my . . .' or 'I can't stand this'.

Extend their listening by asking questions such as: 'How many toys can you remember hearing mentioned in the story?', 'What sort of clothes was Alfie wearing?'

The Ahlbergs' popular Jolly Postman stories, for example, provide opportunities to focus children's listening on the following: naming some of the traditional tale characters visited on the round; the order in which the postman delivered the mail; recalling who received the invitation and who wrote the postcard.

Follow-up
● As the children's confidence and listening skills grow, ask them to detect some of the different ways of talking used on the tape: shouting, whispers, screams and so forth. Can they spot any rhyming or movement words?
● Set greater challenges to increase the children's deduction and inference skills: what kind of person was the giant? How did he get on with other people? What sorts of things was he always saying?

It's not fair!

Focus
Talking through problems and finding solutions by sharing ideas.

What you need
A common classroom problem such as turn-taking.

What to do
This is an activity which works best when you pick up on any concerns or worries the children express at a particular time: 'It's not fair', 'I never have a turn to give out the snacks', 'He has too many turns on the computer' or 'I don't like it when it's noisy all the time.'

When you get the group together, encourage the children to talk about what it feels like when something similar happens to them. Ask how many other people feel like this.

Discuss some possible ways of ironing out these problems. Can the children tell you how they have tried to sort these problems out for themselves? Could they all try some of the ideas which have worked well?

Talk about some class routines that might help resolve the difficulties. You may like to draw on some of the suggestions in the illustration above.

Let's talk

Focus
Talking about what makes a good speaker and listener.

What you need
A flip-chart or chalkboard.

What to do
Talk with the children about what makes a good speaker and listener and tell them they will be working on a poster to help everybody remember.

Discuss with the children some of the practices and devices already used when you are working together: taking turns to speak by putting their hands up, sitting in the talking chair when they have something special to tell other people or taking turns to hold the magic talking stick, so that everybody knows they must listen carefully and not butt in.

Encourage the children to share other ideas about what they think makes a good speaker and listener. Remember to talk about how children can help each other with their speaking and listening, for example, by helping others to make their points clearly without rushing, or saying something positive when somebody has obviously tried hard.

Write some of these ideas on a flip-chart as you go along. At the end of the session you should have a list of points to help the children to become good speakers and listeners: take turns to speak, listen carefully, share ideas, keep trying, say something positive to others.

Follow-up
● Put these aids for speaking and listening on to a poster.
● Choose one of the points as a target for the week. How well do the children think they have done at the end of the week?

Ask me another

Focus
Helping children to ask questions.

What you need
A collection of small objects such as a straw, a necklace, a toy animal, a coin.

Preparation
Ask the children to name and describe the objects in your collection. Focus the talk on shape, colour, what the objects are made of and how we use them.

What to do
Without letting anyone else see, ask the children to take turns choosing an object and hiding it behind their back. The rest of the group should ask them questions to find out what the object is. The child holding the object is allowed to answer only 'yes' or 'no' to the questions. At first, the children will probably just name the object: 'Is it the necklace?' or 'I know, it's the straw.' Help the children to frame questions which give more information such as 'Is it red?', 'Is it longer than my hand?', 'Is it used for eating or drinking?'

When the children have practised asking pertinent questions, set a challenge: how quickly can they find out what the object is? Can they guess it in less than twenty questions?

Follow-up
Use photocopiable page 88 and ask the children to work in pairs. One child 'chooses' a teddy bear without letting his or her partner know which one it is. The partner then asks questions to find out which teddy bear has been chosen, for example, 'Has it got a bow tie?', 'Is the bow tie spotty?'

True or false?

Focus
Talking about fact and fiction.

What you need
A small object to pass round such as a hat, a wooden brick or a toy car.

Preparation
Teach the children to sing these words to the tune of 'London Bridge.'

> Take the car [brick or hat] and
> Pass it round,
> Pass it round, pass it round.
> Take the car and
> Pass it round,
> Who will it be?

What to do
Sit the children in a circle. As they sing the song, they pass the object from hand to hand. Whoever is holding it when the song ends has to say something true about themselves, for example, 'My name is Andreas' or 'I'm wearing red trousers.'

When the others have agreed that this is true, start the song again, passing the object round from where you left off last time. Whoever is holding it next time the song ends also has to say something true about themselves, and so on.

As the children become more confident about what 'true' means, adapt the game to include statements involving both 'true' and 'false'. This time, whoever is left with the object when the song ends, has to say something true or false about themselves or others in the group such as 'I've got brown hair', 'I live on the moon' or 'Gareth has wings.'

16

Musical story

Focus
Listening carefully to a story and using vocal and body sounds as a musical accompaniment.

What you need
Story-books which give a range of obvious animal or vehicle sounds and movements. Try Brian Wildsmith's *Goat's trail* (Oxford University Press), John Burningham's *Mr. Gumpy's Outing* (Puffin) or Pat Hutchins' *Good-night, Owl* (Puffin) or any suitable books you happen to have.

Preparation
Read your selected story and ask the children to listen carefully for sounds made by the animals or vehicles.

What to do
Read the story again. Ask the children to join in with the sounds. Every time the sheep goes 'baa' or the car goes 'vroom-vroom', the children say the words.

Try out a range of body sounds — thigh-slapping, rubbing fingers on the palm of the hand, popping noises and so on. Discuss which of these body sounds the children think would best match the sound words in the book.

Agree which sounds should be a substitute for a pig grunting or a cow mooing, for example. Read the story again while the children listen hard, so they can come in on cue with their body sounds.

Albert's house

Focus
Using a computer program to talk about the layout of houses.

What you need
Albert's House (a BBC computer program).

Preparation
Albert is a mouse. By using different levels of the program, the children can explore his house, play a game of 'hide-and-squeak', and prevent Albert from being caught by the cat.

The first part of the program takes the children inside Albert's house and shows colourful cross-sections of different rooms. There is no text at this stage, and by simply using the cursor arrows, the children can choose where to explore. They can move from room to room, upstairs and downstairs, through doors and into the garden.

What to do
Play the program with the children, discussing the pictures as you go. Help them to identify each of the rooms. Which clues help them to decide where they are? What furnishings are there and what are they used for? Ask the children to consider how Albert's kitchen and bedroom compares with their own at home. Talk about the hall, landing, upstairs and downstairs and how the rooms link together. How can the children be sure they have visited all the rooms?

Follow-up
Encourage the children to explore and discuss the second part of the program, which looks at the rooms in more detail and allows the users to ask for extra information. The minimal text gives such choices as 'Look behind', and 'Look inside', where children may find a sock behind the cushion or dirty water in the bath. Ask the children to talk about what they might find under their own beds or behind the cooker at home. When the children know their way around the program, they could take turns to work with a friend.

Table-top games

Chapter two

Providing children with the opportunity to sit together around a table or other suitable flat surface, and to play games introduces them to important speaking and listening skills: sharing, taking turns, listening carefully, and repeating words and phrases.

A number of the activities in this chapter make use of readily available pictures, either from commercial game packs you will already have (Lotto, Snap, Memory, Happy Families) or which are easily collected from cards, magazines and catalogues.

Encourage the children to bring in their old greetings and celebration cards, and postcards to give the games a personal touch.

A couple of monsters

Focus
Giving clear instructions and listening carefully.

What you need
Two fuzzy-felt boards and felt pieces.

What to do
Children should work in pairs for this activity. Child A makes a simple monster using fuzzy felt without showing it to child B. Child A then describes the monster very clearly so that child B, listening closely, can make one just like it.

The language encouraged will depend on the fuzzy-felt pieces used. Help the children to use words which identify size, colour, shape, position and number of pieces, for example, two red eyes, a big, blue body.

When the two monsters are complete, ask the children to compare them and look for any mismatches.

Follow-up
The same approach can be used with a range of materials to make different pictures and scenes. The instructional language may differ according to the materials used. If the children use construction toys, talk about size, colour, shape and the number of pieces. Plasticine and play dough are good for making snowmen, animals, baskets of fruit or plates of food. Drawing is a useful medium for composite pictures and the positional language entailed in copying them from verbal instructions. Use toy animals for farm or zoo layouts, where the children have to consider the number of animals and position of the fences.

Peep-holes

Focus
Helping children make sensible predictions from an increasing number of clues.

What you need
A peep-hole frame (see illustration), a collection of pictures from old greetings cards, catalogues, postcards or magazines, showing people, places, objects and buildings. The pictures should not be too 'busy'.

What you do
Children should work in pairs or small groups. Put a picture behind the doors face up and close all the doors. In turns, the children open one flap, talk and make suggestions about the clues they have and deduce the possibilities: what kinds of things might it be? For example, one of the peep-holes may reveal part of a wheel, so it might be a form of transport or a hamster's play wheel.

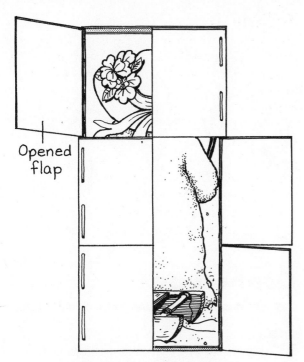

Opened flap

A picture slotted between two sheets of thin card, stapled together along the edges

Tell the children to open another door. Does it confirm or change their original prediction? The children should keep opening the flaps until the whole picture is revealed. Talk about how accurate or otherwise they were. Why were the children misled? Which clues really helped?

Follow-up
This is also a very good game for exploring stereotypes. You could, for example, take a picture of a boy knitting, where the peep-hole shows only the wool and the needles in somebody's hands. Did the children predict that it would turn out to be a boy? Or the picture of a smiling lady with a dog on a lead – did the children expect her to be in a wheelchair?

Making sense

Focus
Developing children's ability to speak in sentences.

What you need
Two groups of pictures, one showing objects and one showing people (make your own or use commercial game cards).

What to do
For this activity, ask the children to work in pairs. Put the two separate piles of cards face down on the table in front of the children. They should take turns to flip over the top card from each pile. Ask the children to look at the two pictures and to link them in a single sentence, for instance, 'The doctor is riding her motorbike.'

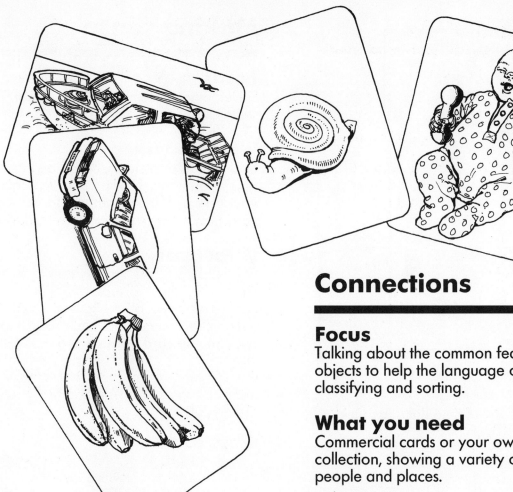

With some children, you could ask for more description of either the doctor or the motorbike: where might she be going? Is there anything special about the motorbike? Talk about how the order of the pictures might alter the sense of what the children say.

Follow-up
Set the children some challenges: what is the longest sentence they can make? Can they give the sentences a touch of fantasy, as in 'The caterpillar leaped over the wall.' Use the cards when helping the children to concentrate on tenses: is it today, yesterday or will it happen tomorrow?

Connections

Focus
Talking about the common features of objects to help the language of classifying and sorting.

What you need
Commercial cards or your own collection, showing a variety of objects, people and places.

What to do
Working with a small group, spread the cards face down on the table. Ask the children to take turns to pick up two cards. Can they make a link between them? Encourage the children to talk about what the objects have in common: the button and the boat may both be blue, for example, or the snail and the coin are both smaller than the children's hands.

You could extend the talk by helping the children to consider how two pictures might belong to the same set: both might be forms of transport, living things or flowers. During the game, if a connection is identified, the child keeps the pair. If not, the pictures are put back face down on the table. Keep going until all possible connections are made.

Talking pictures

Focus
Talking about picture clues, which helps children with story-telling.

What you need
Busy pictures (from story-books and magazines) which give a context such as a picnic scene, a shopping centre, a street party or a religious ceremony.

What to do
Discuss the picture with individual children or a small group. Concentrate on some of the more obvious aspects first: what is going on in the picture? How many people are there and how many different colours can the children see?

Ask the children to look carefully at the position of the people in the picture, and talk about near and far, going into, walking away from and so on.

Ask the children to speculate who the people in the picture might be: a family, friends, shopkeepers, neighbours or police officers. Look for clues that help to identify what the characters might be saying to each other, for instance, big smiles on their faces or pointing fingers.

Follow-up
Turn the picture over and ask the children how much they can remember. Giving the children a focus to concentrate on such as colours, vehicles or the positions of various things in the picture, helps them to recall more detail.

Whatever next!

Focus
Helping children to speculate from a picture stimulus about what might have occurred before and predict what might happen next.

What you need
Pictures from books, posters, wrapping paper etc., depicting a busy scene or action.

What to do
Discuss the picture with a small group to familiarise the children with what is happening in the scene.

Choose a particular aspect of the picture to look at in more detail. For example, the scene could be of a group

of people having a picnic. A girl with an alarmed expression on her face might be running away from the picnic basket. Now ask the children what might have led up to this incident. Why might the girl be running away? Have a swarm of bees descended on the doughnuts? Or is she trying to make a quick get away before someone spots her helping herself to Dad's favourite pastie?

What do the children think is going to happen next? Encourage them to make sensible suggestions, in keeping with the context of the picture (it is an interesting idea, but it is unlikely that she is about to go Christmas shopping).

Follow-up
Using photocopiable page 89, talk to the children about each picture in turn. What is going on here? What led up to this? What might happen next?

Jigsaws

Focus
Mathematical language, especially position, shape and fit.

What you need
A collection of old postcards, pencils and scissors.

What to do
Keep the group small or work with individual children. Give each child a picture and discuss it, so they know what their finished jigsaw should look like.

Ask the children to draw a few lines on the back of the picture and cut along them (see illustration). With the picture side up, the children should now jumble up the pieces and re-assemble the picture. As they do this, discuss shapes that have straight lines, corners and

curves, and pieces which join up or leave a space. Do they need to flip them over or turn the pieces round to make them fit? Help them to recognise clues from the colours and context: could the blue pieces, for example, belong to the sky or a jumper?

Follow-up
● Jumble up three simple jigsaws. Ask the children to sort the pieces out into three separate pictures, using criteria such as whether the pieces have glitter on them, looking for shades of the same colour that might belong together, or looking for parts of characters.
● Use more complex pictures or the children's own drawings and increase the number of pieces.

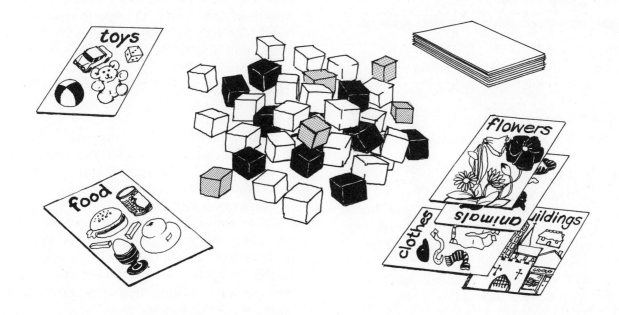

Does it belong?

Focus
Talking about objects which belong to the same categories.

What you need
Cue cards showing a single word, a picture or montage (use catalogue pictures), cubes or building bricks to use as counters.

What to do
Play this game with two or three children. Look at and talk about the cue cards to make sure the children are familiar with the set headings.

Put the cubes or bricks in the middle of the table and the cue cards face down in a pile. The first child picks up a card and names something belonging to that set. For example, if the cue card shows the set is 'toys', the child has to name something which is a toy (kite, ball, etc.). If the item is accepted by the other players as part of the set, the child picks up a cube. The card is then passed on to the next child in the game, who has in turn to name something else belonging to the same set (doll, train set, etc.). If this is accepted by the others, the child picks up a cube, too. The game ends when all the counters are used up or when the children run out of ideas.

If a particular child is unable to name something belonging to the set, he or she should say so and pass the card on to the next player, without taking a cube. When the game ends, the children can make a tower with their counters and compare heights to see who has won that round. The next round starts with a child picking up a new cue card.

Follow-up
Using photocopiable page 90, ask the children to name the set and identify one thing that does not belong to the collection ('the odd one out'). Ask them to give reasons for their choice.

25

Happy Families

Focus
Helping children to formulate their own responses to a specific question.

What you need
A pack of Happy Family cards.

Preparation
Play a game of Happy Families in the usual way. This introduces the children to skills such as recognising categories (the names of the different families), spotting incomplete sets ('I need to ask for Master and Mrs Bunn') and how to ask questions ('Have you got Mr Stamp the postman?').

What to do
Play another game of Happy Families, this time helping the children to change the form of questioning. Tell them to

pretend they have a message for a member of the family or want to invite one of them to tea. Instead of saying, 'Have you got Mr Dose the chemist?', they should say: 'Is Miss/Mr/Mrs Dose in, please?' If whoever is being asked has the card, they say 'yes' in the usual way and hand it over. If they have not, the responses might go something like this:

    'Is Miss Brush in, please?'
    'No, sorry.'
    'Where has she gone?'
    'She's gone to the park'.

When the children have practised this version of the game, ask them to think more carefully about where a particular character might have gone in connection with the family occupation – for example, Miss Brush might be out painting Mr Stamp's door or Miss Dough could be delivering bread to the shop.

Forwards and backwards

Focus
Helping the children to use the language of reasoning.

What you need
A familiar track game which has bonuses and forfeits.

What to do
Play a track game the children know well. But, this time, tell the children that when they land on bonus and forfeit squares, they have to think up reasons or explain why they are moving backwards, forwards, having another go or missing a turn.

If the children are playing a Postman Pat game, for example, the board instructions might say 'Miss a turn, you've lost Jess.' Discuss why losing Jess might make Pat late — perhaps he would have to stop the van and look for her. Or, if a bonus square tells them to move on three spaces or have another turn, the reasons could be that Pat has finished his round and will not have to stop the van any more or has no heavy birthday presents to deliver today.

If your Postman Pat game simply says things like 'Miss a turn' or 'Have another go', ask the children to make up their own reasons for this.

Spot the sequence

Focus
Recognising and describing important characteristics of objects and using them to make a sequence or pattern.

What you need
Collections of objects to put into an easily recognised sequence such as leaves, buttons, crayons, shells and cotton reels.

What to do
Discuss with the children some of the objects from your collection, helping them to recognise and describe useful characteristics. With buttons, for example, discuss different colours, sizes, patterning and the fact that some have two holes while others have four.

When the children are really comfortable with describing the characteristics of the objects, ask them to make a simple sequence (see illustration).

It helps if you talk the sequence through as the children are placing the objects in the pattern: two holes/four holes or big/small/small/big and so on.

The describing words may change

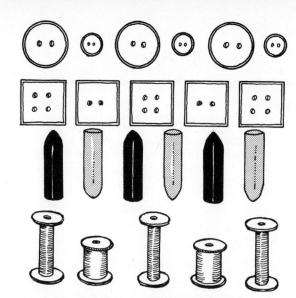

according to your collection. With crayons, you could talk about colour, thickness and length. Shells could be sequenced by shape, pattern and size.

Follow-up
Make a simple sequence yourself and, unseen by the children, take one object away and ask them to describe what is missing.

Quack, toot, bang

Focus
Recognising and recalling sounds associated with objects.

What you need
A set of pictures (from Lotto, Snap, any commercial game or cut from pictures and magazines); these should show single objects and must include things that make sounds such as animals, an alarm clock, a whistle.

What to do
Working with three or four children, sort the pictures into two sets, separating those objects which make sounds from

the ones that do not. As the children are sorting, encourage them to imitate the sound associated with each object or animal (duck goes quack, quack, hammer goes bang, bang and so on).

Depending on what you want to get out of the game, you could either leave it at that or go on to consider things such as leaves scrunching or fish blowing bubbles.

Follow-up
Use the cards to play a game of sound lotto. It helps if you sort the cards into sets such as animal sounds, kitchen sounds (washing machine, kettle, electric mixer) or information sounds (alarm clock, doorbell, car horn).

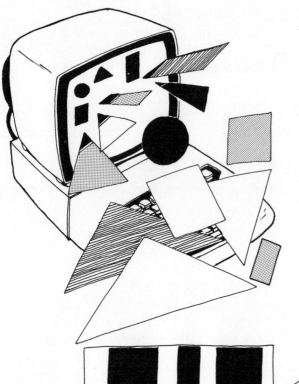

Build

Focus
Using a computer program to help children to talk about the properties of plane shapes and to share their ideas.

What you need
Nursery computer program (Archimedes) or any other program which allows children to work with plane shapes.

Preparation
Part of the program called 'Build' allows children to select plane shapes (circle, triangle, square) from a bank displayed on the screen to make their own pictures.

What to do
This activity will work best if the children take turns to work in pairs. Drawing on the children's experience of using fuzzy felt- and card shapes, talk with them about the properties of shapes and how they fit together. Ask them questions such as 'How can you make a pointed roof?', 'Which shape fits exactly on top of the large square?', 'Are the two posts the same height?'

Prompt the children to share their ideas and to give each other directions to predict, for example, how many more tiles they will need to make the path reach the house and which shape might fit into the tiny space.

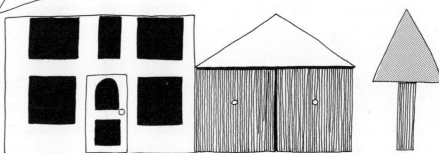

Play house and role-play

Chapter three

Role-play is an invaluable tool for developing speaking and listening skills. Early years children need time and space to explore their own world — what they know about already and what things might feel like from another person's point of view.

Free play is extremely important, but effective speaking and listening can be fostered by structured play, too: introducing simple props, setting a challenge or joining in yourself when it seems appropriate.

You do not need to have a sophisticated play house. The activities in this chapter will work just as well if you use a curtain and some boxes to give the children a feeling of a special place where they can play make-believe.

Phone a friend

Focus
Chatting socially on the telephone.

What you need
A yoghurt-pot telephone (see illustration), a walkie-talkie, an old telephone or a toy one.

Preparation
Let the children practise taking it in turns to speak and listen by using a walkie-talkie or a yoghurt-pot telephone. Help them to understand that it is impossible to hold a conversation if both people are speaking at the same time.

What to do
Tell the children to pretend they are going to ring up a friend to invite them over to play. Discuss the kinds of things they might talk about during their telephone conversation.

Explain that it is helpful to begin their conversation with a polite opening sentence such as, 'Hello, is Grace there, please?' They could go on to chat about some of the things they enjoyed last time they played together and exchanging ideas about what else they could do: 'Shall we play our aliens game in the den again?', 'I've got a brilliant new game. Do you want to play it?' Older children could discuss details such as times, dates, favourite food and travel arrangements.

Follow-up
Provide the children with other contexts in which to practise conversation: ringing a friend who has moved away or sharing family news with grandma.

I'm not sure about . . .

Focus
Using puppets to help children talk about and act out potentially difficult situations.

What you need
A selection of simple hand- or finger puppets.

What to do
Children often find it easier to talk about their personal worries and problems through role-play with puppets. Using the puppets yourself to begin with, rehearse some potentially worrying situations, such as delivering a message to somebody else in the building. Feed in questions and appropriate responses to the children.

The children might ask things such as 'What shall I say when I get there?' 'Do you have to wait?' 'What if I get lost on the way?' As the children talk these issues through, diffuse their worries and correct

Once upon a time

Focus
Imaginative talk through puppets based on characters from traditional tales.

What you need
A selection of puppets to represent some characters used in traditional tales.

Preparation
Ask the children to recall and describe some of the characters they have met in traditional tales: princes and princesses, dragons, giants, witches, wizards, Brer Rabbit and Anansi. Focus the talk on the kinds of things such characters usually say and do. Giants may have a big, deep voice or a refrain ('Fee fi fo fum') and have lots of mishaps. Wizards may be helpful and Anansi is a trickster. Are princes always brave as they rush around rescuing people?

What to do
Using the puppets, give the children a very simple scenario such as 'The prince finds the shy giant hiding in a castle.' As the children are enacting this scene, encourage them to imagine how the main characters would act and what they might say to each other. For example, when the prince first comes across the giant, what would he say to himself? How would he persuade such a shy giant to talk to him? Would he tackle the situation himself or send for his knights? Why is the giant hiding in the tower in the first place?

Follow-up
Talk to the children about the picture on photocopiable page 91 and ask them what the characters might be saying or thinking in the bubbles.

any misinformation they may have gathered.

Other common worries you could discuss through role-play are: a visit from the school dentist, having school dinners for the first time, a show-and-tell session or assembly presentation.

Follow-up
Make puppets available in the play area for children to use when they need to talk about outside issues and other personal concerns: the birth of a new baby, moving house or bereavement.

children about how various characters get on with each other and help them to remember where stories have been set before. Discuss where the children could send their favourite characters this time — a train journey, a shopping trip or a carnival, perhaps.

What to do
Ask the children to create their own story-lines, using the puppets or simple props to help them. If the children get stuck or their talk becomes repetitive, inject a challenge such as: 'Who do you think your character might meet?' 'What kinds of things happen to Meg so that she needs to make a spell?' 'Do the spells work well or do they end in disaster?'

Catch-phrases

Focus
Identifying words or phrases used by people the children know well and using them in role-play.

What you need
No special requirements.

What to do
In a small group, discuss some of the people the children know well such as teachers, childminders, playgroup leaders, the school cook or crossing patrol people. Encourage the children to share their ideas, brainstorm words, phrases and mannerisms which are characteristic of these people. These might include 'What's the magic word?', as the children take their dinner or 'Well done, sunshine', as they clear away.

Choose some examples which are familiar to all the children in the group and ask them to act them out.

Meg and Mog go west

Focus
Story-telling and developing imaginative language through characterisation.

What you need
Hand puppets or simple props to link in with story-series characters such as Helen Nicoll's and Jan Pienkowski's Meg and Mog, Susanna Gretz's Bears, Judith Kerr's Mog the cat or James Berry's Anancy the trickster.

Preparation
Choose a favourite series and tell the children they are going to take these well-known characters into a new situation. Help them to recall and describe what particular characters are like. For example, how does Meg dress? Is she friendly, kind, funny? Talk to the

Dragon's lair

Focus
Using your play house or drama area to create opportunities for imaginative talk.

What you need
Drapes, an assortment of different-sized cardboard boxes.

What to do
Let the children transform your play house or drama area into a dragon's lair. Give the children a few simple props such as drapes and boxes. Use things which can be moved easily by the children so that individuals have a chance to explore their own imaginative ideas.

As the children are playing, encourage them to describe their dragon's lair by asking questions such as the following: 'Where is it — in a cave, on top of a mountain or under the sea?', 'Is it big and airy or cramped and dark?', 'Does the dragon need any furniture?', 'Is there a spyhole?'

Follow-up
Let the children create other fantastical situations, for example, an enchanted forest, a robot's moon buggy or a wizard's cave.

Acting out

Focus
Understanding and interpreting gestures, which is an important part of speaking and listening.

What you need
Pictures of busy situations such as shopping, a picnic, a playground, a swimming pool, a fairground or a party.

Preparation
Discuss your chosen pictures with the children. Help them to identify and describe the locations and what the people in the pictures are doing. Focus the talk on the body movements and actions involved. Tell the children they are going to play a game without words and let them practise making the sorts of exaggerated movements needed in mime.

What to do
Look more closely at two of the pictures you have chosen such as shopping and a picnic. Practise together three to five actions associated with each picture: pushing the trolley, taking tins and packets off the shelves, paying the cashier; spreading out the rug, opening the hamper, eating a messy roll — or anything else the children suggest. Let the children take turns to act out part of a situation, while the rest of the group try to guess which picture it belongs to.

Follow-up
● Give the children three different situation pictures to look at. One child should act out some associated movements, while the others guess to which picture the actions belong.
● Play the same game, but this time the child chosen to mime can see the pictures. Can the rest of the group work out the situation?

TV news

Focus
Evaluation of children's speech by themselves and others.

What you need
A simple television screen or frame (see illustration).

Preparation
As a different way of telling their news, ask the children to pretend to be television newsreaders. To help them feel confident about talking on their own, let the children practise in front of an audience of one or two. What they choose to tell their viewers may be very simple at first, perhaps no more than a sentence such as 'I'm going to have tea at Niki's house today.'

What to do
Once the children have practised, ask them to think carefully about how well they have done with their newsreading, before you ask the 'viewers' to say what they thought was good about it.

Encourage them to consider how clearly the 'newsreaders' spoke; were they too fast or too slow? Were they looking in the right direction? Did they get the words in the right order so that it made sense? Older or more able children will be supplying the audience with longer news stories. Ask them to consider the sequence of their stories. Could other people follow it, or did they flit about too much? Have they got their message across? Would facial expressions help?

The 'viewers' can act as the newsreaders' 'critical friends'. Can they say what they especially like about the performance and make helpful suggestions for making it even better? Help them to use the 'control knobs' on the television screen to give feedback to the newsreader by adjusting the volume or the speed control.

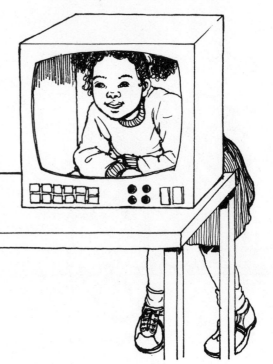

What's up, doc?

Focus
Encouraging children to be aware of, and use, different types of talk in a particular social context.

What you need
A play house or a play area, any simple hospital-type props you already have or which the children can make themselves such as charts, message pads, bleepers and medical instruments.

Preparation
Tell the children the play house is going to be turned into an area they would see in a hospital and that they are going to pretend to be some of the people they might meet there. Discuss any first-hand experiences of hospitals the children may already have or show them pictures and books.

Talk about different people and the kinds of jobs they do: doctors, nurses, patients, cleaners, porters, receptionists and paramedics. What kinds of things would these people say to each other? Choose one aspect of hospital life to focus on, for example, visiting time, the doctor's round, the operating theatre or the X-ray department. Each of these provides opportunities for different kinds of talk.

Take the outpatients department, for example. Discuss the people the children will need to have in their play house: patients waiting to be seen, a receptionist, doctors whizzing in and out, and nurses.

What to do
Let the children play freely in their new outpatients department. As they are playing, encourage them to invent conversations. What would the patients be saying to each other as they wait to see the doctor? How does the doctor talk to his patients? What might the receptionist say to the patient?

Develop other forms of talk by suggesting that some of the characters might need message pads, case notes, appointment slips, charts or an intercom. Get into role yourself now and again to give the children a clearer idea of what they could be saying to each other.

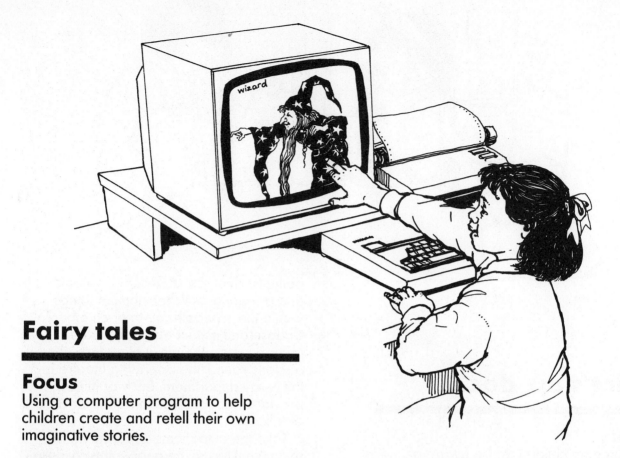

Fairy tales

Focus
Using a computer program to help children create and retell their own imaginative stories.

What you need
A computer program such as *Fairy Tales* or *Old McDonald's Farm* (BBC), which enables children to draw on picture banks to create their own stories.

Preparation
Both programs mentioned above are designed to allow children to make their own story-books, using a bank of pictures and text. However, it is not necessary to use the written language in the early stages. In *Fairy tales*, the 'library' of over 70 pictures includes people (girl, boy, knight), fantastical characters (dragon, wizard, princess), animals and objects (bright star, flying saucer, chairs, fountain, ship, basket, etc.). The pictures can be moved around the screen, added to, removed and made to overlap, to create stimulating picture scenes.

What to do
In pairs or in a small group, explain to the children they are going to make a story using the pictures. As you familiarise the children with some of the pictures, develop their imaginative language by talking about the characters. Is the wizard friendly, helpful, angry, accident-prone? Where might he live? Who else could be in the story?

At first, the children might like to create a simple visual scenario to use as an aid to their story-telling. As they become more confident, encourage them to move characters on and off the screen, and add objects to embellish their creations. Ask them to retell their stories to each other or to a group.

Construction area

Chapter four

This is the area where children build and explore, using large and small construction toys, junk materials and robotic toys if you have them. You can develop children's constructions by using them with play mats, toy animals and people, and theme kits such as vehicles, and farm or zoo animals.

Story-telling and imaginative play are stimulated by constructional work as children use their models to retell a familiar story or create their own scenarios.

Copy me

Focus
Practising giving and receiving instructions.

What you need
Any constructional or building toys such as bricks, interlocking cubes, junk boxes and cardboard tubes.

What to do
Put the children into pairs and give each child in the pair the same constructional toys. Child A should then build a simple tower or wall without letting child B see. When she has finished, she must describe carefully how the model was made, so that child B can make one just like it.

As the children are giving their instructions, encourage them to talk about the size and colour of each piece used and where it has been placed, for instance, 'Take the big, red brick first and put it on top of the long, thin, yellow one.' The children will have to remember to tell their partners how many pieces to use and whether they should be placed side by side or on top of each other.

Compare the two models and discuss any differences. Ask the children to change over so they both practise giving and listening to instructions.

Follow-up
After practice, the children could make more complicated models such as robots, lorries with six wheels or shopping trolleys.

Prop up a story

Focus
Retelling a story with the aid of props.

What you need
Construction toys, a favourite book such as the *Stanley and Rhoda* stories by Rosemary Wells.

What to do
Help the children to decide which book they would like to use. Tell them they are going to make a model of something which is mentioned a lot in the book, so they can use it to help them retell the story with a friend.

To assist the children in deciding which prop to make, discuss with them who the main characters are and what happens to them. There is no need to make each of the main characters: these can be represented by a soft toy or a LEGO person.

Take one of the Stanley and Rhoda stories, for example. The children might decide to make a simple model of the wagon which was filled with rocks and dragged up the hill just before Rhoda gets stung by a bee. The wagon then becomes the main prop used to help retell the story.

Discuss with the children how they are going to make their model wagon. How big will it be? Is there room for Rhoda as well as the 'rocks' (LEGO bricks, etc.)? Will it have a handle, so that it can be pulled up the hill more easily?

Help the children to retell the story so that the props complement the action.

Follow-up
Try the same approach with other stories, for example, Pamela Allen's *Who Sank the Boat?* (Puffin) — the children could make the boat and use toy farm animals to retell the story; or Shirley Hughes' *An Evening at Alfie's* (Picture Lions) — they could make buckets and bowls or beds for Alfie and Annie Rose.

Three bears, three chairs

Focus
Comparative language and encouraging children to evaluate their own work.

What you need
Construction toys and soft toys to represent the three bears.

Preparation
Read or tell the children the story of the three bears — the version by Jonathan Langley (Picture Lions) is a popular one. As you read, ask them to listen out for words connected with size — wider, bigger, biggest, largest of all and so on.

What to do
Tell the children they are going to make bowls, chairs and beds in different sizes for Mummy, Daddy and Baby Bear. It may help the children to get the idea of 'fit' if you give them some toys to represent the three different-sized bears.

As the children are building, help them to use words which compare – wide, wider, widest; big, bigger, biggest; short, shorter, shortest.

When the children have finished their models, help them to talk about how successful they have been: is the bed long/wide enough for Daddy Bear to sleep in? Is the chair too small for Mummy Bear? Is the bowl just the right size for Baby Bear?

Relate sizes to the children's own experience and encourage responses such as the following: 'My bed is bigger than my sister's cot', 'It's not as wide as Mummy and Daddy's bed.'

Follow-up
Cut out the pictures on photocopiable page 92 with the children and help them to match each bear to the appropriate-sized chair, bed and bowl. Talk about too big, too small and just the right size.

Faulty towers

Focus
Developing technical language through constructing towers.

What you need
Suitable materials to build towers – paper cups, cotton reels, cardboard tubes and boxes, loose and interlocking bricks.

What to do
Work with a small group. Ask the children to build a tower using some of the materials listed above. As they are building, talk about which shapes stack well and which ones do not; whether they have edges and straight or curved surfaces. Encourage the children to try different ways of stacking, using words such as flip it over, turn it round, upright, sides, ends and flat.

Discuss with the children how the objects fit together: are there spaces between them? How many bricks are needed to fill them? Let the children explore and discuss different ways of making paper cups fit together, for example, slotting them inside each other to make a short, strong tower, making a pyramid or alternating the tops and bottoms (see illustration).

Follow-up

Choose one building material and set a challenge for the children such as, 'Build the tallest or strongest tower you can with 15 or 20 bricks. Why did the tallest one fall over?'

Neighbours

Focus

Building on the children's experience of everyday conversations.

What you need

A selection of boxes and cartons to represent houses in a street, LEGO people or soft toys to act as the occupants.

Preparation

The children are going to make a simple cardboard street based on their own neighbourhood. Discuss different types of houses they may recognise: terraced, blocks of flats, a flat above a shop and detached dwellings. Consider the kinds of people living in the children's own streets: families, young and older couples, and people living alone. Use LEGO people or soft toys to represent them.

What to do

Ask the children to work in pairs to construct their street. Talk to them about the people they know and have spoken to in their own area — family and friends, next-door neighbours, childminders or the babysitter. Where do the children meet these people? Do they have conversations over the garden fence, in the street outside the house, on the way to school or when they visit for tea?

Ask the children to consider the kinds of things neighbours say to them. Examples might include: 'Hello, how are you today?', 'You'll be late for school if you stand around talking to me', 'Are you coming out to play?', 'John's riding his bike on the road again, instead of on the pavement.' Use the children's box street and toy characters to practise conversational language.

Follow-up

Use the model street to encourage the children to practise conversations between other neighbourhood characters, for example, the old lady talking to her dog or the milkman on his rounds.

On the road

Focus
Talking about the properties of vehicles.

What you need
Toy vehicles, any constructional toys with wheels, a simple road (a play mat if you have one, a paper road or any flat surface).

Preparation
Tell the children they are going to make some vehicles to play with. Look at some of the toys you already have and talk with the children about the sorts of things they have in common: size, wheels, doors and so on. If your collection contains an ambulance or a police car, draw on the children's experience to discuss other vehicles which help us, such as fire engines and delivery vans. Ask the children to consider whether everything that has wheels goes on a roadway. What about prams and pushchairs, bicycles and shopping trolleys?

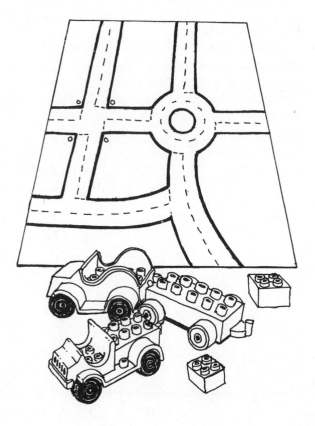

What to do
Help the children to decide which vehicles they would like to make to add to the collection. As the children are building, discuss features such as the number of wheels or doors. Is their vehicle intended for carrying passengers or goods? If it is designed to transport loads, will it need sides and a roof or a tipping device? Talk about the added extras special vehicles like fire engines and ambulances need such as hose-pipes and ladders.

Follow-up
Use the models on the roadway. Would the children like to add special junctions, parking places or a one-way street? Is there plenty of room for tankers and lorries to turn round?

Box it up

Focus
Language associated with solving practical problems.

What you need
Construction toys.

What to do
Set a challenge for the children to solve, based on a character from a traditional tale. Examples could include making a lunch box for one of Snow White's seven

dwarfs or making a box for Prince Charming to keep the glass slipper safe as he travels the land looking for Cinderella.

When the children have decided which character to help, talk about how big the box will need to be (use bricks or beads as pretend food). Will it have sides to stop everything falling out? Is it deep enough? Does the box need a lid in case it rains? Talk about how the box will be carried. Would a handle help?

Encourage the children to exchange ideas and help each other to make their containers work better.

Follow-up
● Using photocopiable page 93, ask the children to match up the objects to the best-sized container. Talk about height, width, length, shape and size.
● As the children become more confident about problem solving, you could set a more open-ended challenge. Can they think of a way to help Jack carry his loot down the beanstalk and still have his hands free? Or devise another means of making a quick escape — for example, a chute, a skateboard, a helicopter or a crane?

Where's Spot?

Focus
Developing talk by using simple programmable toys.

What you need
A Roamer or a Valiant Turtle (or equivalent), a hat, a cushion, a box and a soft toy to represent Spot the dog.

Preparation
Set up a course for the Roamer to travel, and hide 'Spot' under either the hat, the box or the cushion as shown in the illustration.

What you do
Working with a small group, tell the children Spot is hiding in the garden and they are going to ask the Roamer to help find him. Ask the children to decide where to look first. Do they think he is hiding under the hat, the box or the cushion?

If they decide to look under the box first, for example, tell them to stand the Roamer on the 'garden path' opposite the box. Encourage the children to predict how many steps ('units') they think the Roamer will need to go. Ask them

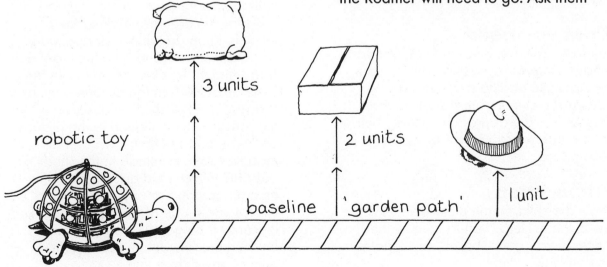

robotic toy

3 units

2 units

1 unit

baseline   'garden path'

which direction it needs to travel (forwards, backwards, left or right).

When the children have agreed on directions, tell them to program the Roamer accordingly, talking all the time about the order of commands and the importance of giving clear, step-by-step instructions. Let the children try out their programmed instructions and discuss what happens. Has the Roamer gone too far or not far enough? Did it travel in the direction they wanted? How many units did it travel?

If it has not worked as the children predicted, discuss what instructions they need to change, for instance, if it went too far last time, what should they try this time?

When the Roamer reaches the box, ask the children to look underneath. Is Spot there? If not, they should go back to the garden path and choose somewhere else to search.

Just like the picture

Focus
Talking about making models from a picture stimulus.

What you need
Toy farm animals, fences, gates, trees and sheds from a farmyard kit, construction toys to make additions if needed, farmyard pictures from story-books or magazines. The approach outlined below can be easily adapted for any picture you choose.

Preparation
Show the children the picture and discuss it with them. Help them to identify the fences, fields, gates, barns, sheds, paths and animals.

What to do
Ask the children to work in pairs to make a model of the farm picture. Talk about what they are going to make first, and how to exchange ideas and divide tasks with their partner.

As the children are making their models, keep drawing their attention back to the picture to help them get a good match. Talk with them about the number of fields in the picture, sizes and shapes. Can the children describe where the fences are positioned in the picture and where to put their own on the model? Are the animals in the sheds or outside? Which field are the sheep in — next to the cows or behind the barn? Is the tractor in one of the fields or parked in front of the gate? Compare the finished models with the picture and discuss any differences.

Sand and water

Chapter five

This area is anywhere where you can contain sand and water. The activities suggested in this chapter will work if you use plastic bowls, the sink, outside pools and pits or indoor trays.

It is a good idea to limit the number of objects or the type of equipment you provide for sand and water play. Structuring the materials in this way helps direct the children to different kinds of language. Quality play and therefore on-task speaking and listening will happen because the materials are new and interesting, and pose fresh challenges for the children to discuss — even if you cannot be with them all the time.

Wet and dry

Focus
Reporting observations to a group.

What you need
A selection of small objects: a sponge, a feather, soap, a pebble, greaseproof paper and pieces of chamois leather; water in small containers. Having two of each of these objects makes it easier for children to compare and talk about them when first dry and then wet.

Preparation
With a small group, take one dry object at a time and ask the children to look at it carefully. Discuss its colour, size, shape, texture and any patterns they may notice.

Ask the children to put the object in water. When it is thoroughly wet, take it out again and ask them to study it closely, and talk about what it looks like compared to the dry one.

Do the same with some of the other objects. Explain to the children that they are going to tell the other children about the changes they noticed.

What to do
Just before the group reports back on what they found out, help them to recap on what they did, and what they found out. Keep the report-back session short and simple. Help the children to recall some of the changes they noticed and encourage them to speculate about why these changes occurred: when Kelly put her pebble in the water she noticed that the colours changed — can you tell us about that? Oliver was surprised that the sponge was much heavier when it was wet — could you tell the other children about it, please?

Tell the rest of the children to listen very carefully so they can decide which objects they'd like to talk about when it is their turn. Have they thought of any others that might be interesting to compare when wet and dry?

Sieve it!

Focus
Talking about how to match tools to specific jobs.

What you need
A tea strainer, a flour sprinkler, a colander, a kitchen spatula with holes, a toaster grill, a garden sieve, a salad shaker, dry sand.

Preparation
The children should work in pairs so they can take turns to hold the sieve while the other pours the sand. Using dry sand, the children can explore and talk about what happens when they pour it into the different sieves. Help them to discuss why some sieves allow the sand to gush out, while with others it trickles through. Encourage the children to experiment with different ways of using the sieves: shaking, tapping the sides, rubbing the sand through with their hands.

What to do
Add things to the sand for the children to separate out with the sieves. You could start with things such as model animals, twigs, large shells and so on. Ask the children to look closely and describe what happens. Now give them some smaller objects like pebbles, peas and small shells to separate. What do they notice?

Discuss which sieves do a particular job well. Which objects go through the sieves and why? Will any of the things the children are trying to separate go through all the sieves? What were the easiest or most difficult objects to separate?

Castles in the sand

Focus
Talking about problem-solving and sharing ideas.

What you need
Pictures of castles from books and magazines, damp sand, sand tools.

Preparation
Show the children the pictures and discuss some of the architectural features of the castles such as windows, towers, turrets and arches.

What to do
In pairs, let the children choose one of the castle pictures to make in the sand. Help them to decide together how they are going to make different-shaped towers with their hands. Can they make short, fat towers and tall, thin ones? Can they suggest what they might use to make the job easier, for example, buckets and

moulds? Encourage the children to talk through their ideas about how to make a tunnel, moat or doorway without the sand caving in. Can they help each other to find ways of preventing the tall towers from falling over? Talk about using twigs, shells or stones to represent features such as windows and flags.

Bubbles

Focus
Talking about a challenge and sharing ideas.

What you need
A sponge, a squeezy bottle, a straw, a piece of plastic tubing, a hand whisk, water in large bowls.

Preparation
Give a small group of children some plain water and no other equipment, and ask them if they can think of a way of making bubbles. Let them try out their ideas, which might include swirling the water around with their hands or blowing across the top of it.

What to do
Ask the children to discuss and try out their ideas for making bubbles with some of the equipment listed above. Encourage them to explain to each other and demonstrate how they made the bubbles with the whisk or squeezy bottle, for example. Even if all the children in the group managed to make bubbles with the same piece of equipment, they may well have achieved it in different ways. Keep encouraging them to exchange ideas.

Follow-up
Try adding washing-up liquid in varying concentrations. Do warn them not to drink the bubbly mixture! Let the children experiment with different bubble-makers. What observations can the children make now? Are there more bubbles? Are their shapes different?

Pattern-makers

Focus
Talking about reasons why — the early stages of logic and deduction.

What you need
Damp sand, combs, rakes, sticks, a potato masher, old construction bricks and toy vehicles, a fir cone, feathers.

Preparation
Let the children play in the damp sand with some of the above items, exploring the kinds of marks they can make. Can they describe the connection between a straight print and the patterns created by dragging an item? Discuss how they made shallow and deep patterns. What do the children notice when they rake the sand in one direction and then another?

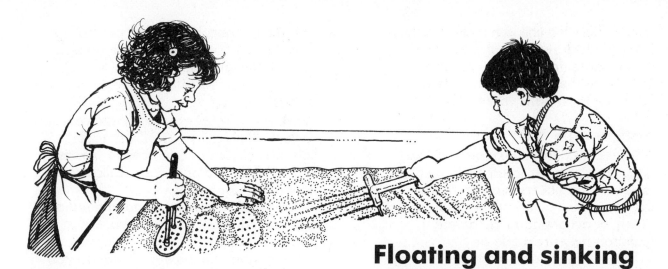

What to do

Put the children into pairs. Using two of the objects (e.g. the potato masher and the Duplo brick), child A makes a pattern in the damp sand while child B looks away. Child A puts the print-makers used to one side but does not hide them. Child B tries to match the prints to the print maker: which two objects made the marks?

Help the children to make sensible deductions by comparing the shape and pattern of the objects with the prints left in the sand. Ask questions like: what sorts of things have we got in our collection that might make marks like that? Has it made big or small prints, sharp lines, dots? Build on responses such as: 'It must be this one, because . . .'

Try the activity with different pairs of print-makers and increase the number of objects when the children are more confident about making deductions in this way.

Follow-up

Using photocopiable page 94, talk to the children about the pattern-makers at the top of the page (car, cat, bicycle, etc.). Ask the children to match the prints to the print-makers, using the language of reasoning, for example, 'It can't be, because . . .' or 'It must be . . .'

Floating and sinking

Focus

Talking about sorting.

What you need

A collection of objects which will float or sink: a cork, a shell, squeezy bottles, a plastic food tray, a large, empty tin (floaters); metal cutlery, Plasticine, a paper-clip, a badge, a coin (sinkers); water in large bowls.

Preparation

Discuss your collection with the group, concentrating particularly on similarities and differences. Talk about whether the items have holes, the materials they are made of, colour, shape, size and weight. Talking about and naming characteristics may help the children to give reasons why objects sink or float. Ask the children to predict what might happen to the various articles as they put them into the water.

What to do

Ask the children to watch carefully and talk about what they notice as the objects are put in the water: do they stay on the surface? Do they sink straight away or after some time? Do all the sinkers go down the same way or do some sink at an angle?

Now help the children sort the objects into groups drawing on the earlier observations, for instance, 'These made bubbles as they went down', 'These floated', 'These sank very quickly.'

Follow-up
• After considerable exploration and discussion, some children might be able to sort all the sinkers in different ways: things that sink quickly/things that sink slowly or according to the different materials they are made of.
• The children might sort the floaters by size, materials or whether they float on the surface or just underneath.

Making waves

Focus
Talking about what might happen if . . .

What you need
Large and small objects to drop into the water: matchsticks, small and large pebbles, corks, straws; water in large bowls.

Preparation
Talk to the children about where they have seen ripples and waves before: in the bath, at the seaside, in the sink. Ask them to try making ripples and waves with their fingers and hands, prompting them to describe what they are doing and what might happen next.

What to do
Work with a small group. Let the water settle. Tell the children to drop a small, light object such as a matchstick into the middle of the water surface. Talk about how the water moves.

Ask the children open-ended questions such as 'What do you think would happen if we dropped the matchstick in at the edge of the bowl?', 'What do you think will happen to the patterns in the water now?'

Try dropping a pebble into the water and ask the children to consider if the effects will be the same. Invite them to suggest other ways of making a ripple with the pebble and try out their ideas. What do they think might happen if they drop it into the water from higher up or put it in very slowly and carefully? Encourage the children all the time to model their questions on your own and to give reasons for their ideas: 'I think it will make a big wave because . . .'

Capability Brown

Focus
Collaborative talk and planning.

What you need
Pictures of gardens, damp sand, stones, fir cones, shells, twigs, small pieces of wood, tips of evergreens, moss, a small clump of grass.

Preparation
Look at the pictures and discuss the various features that might be found in gardens: play space, pathways, seats, ponds and fountains, raised flowerbeds and so on. Tell the children they are going to work with a partner to plan and make their own gardens in the sand.

What to do
Discuss the children's plans for their own garden layout. Which of the features you have just been talking about do they think they might try in theirs? Encourage them to listen to each other's suggestions about what to include and how to make it.

If they decide on a pond, for example, what sorts of containers do they think they might use? Where might they put the paths or the rockery and how will they prevent the 'soil' from falling down all the time? Talk about what they might use for the trees and bushes.

Ask the children to decide if they will make everything together or if one of them will concentrate on a certain part while their partner is busy with another.

Hills and valleys

Focus
Talking about the properties of sand as the children explore through touch.

What you need
Dry sand, pourers or funnels such as jugs, teapots, paper cones, different-sized tubes.

What to do
Tell the children to build a simple landscape in the sand for their toy animals or construction kit characters. You could suggest a safari park, farm

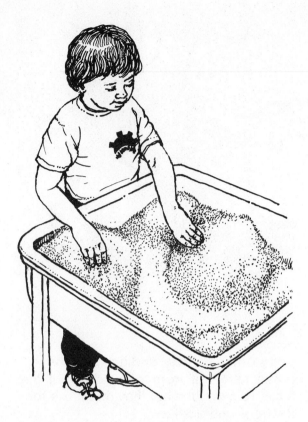

Fun at the seaside

Focus
Using sand and water to help retell stories.

What you need
Damp sand, stones, shells, sand tools, a book with a strong sand-and-water theme, for example, Susanna Gretz's *Bears Who Went to the Seaside* (A. & C. Black), Eric Hill's *Spot Goes on Holiday* (Puffin) or Shirley Hughes' *Lucy and Tom at the Seaside* (Puffin).

Preparation
Choose a seaside book to read and discuss with the children. Tell them they are going to choose one part of the story to model in the sand.

What to do
Let the children decide which part of the story they would like to recreate. They might choose the part they found the most amusing or wish they could do themselves.

Take *Lucy and Tom at the Seaside*, for example. The children could decide to build a beautiful sand castle or make a face with rows of teeth and seaweed hair. Or they could use some water in a container and make a rock pool like the one Lucy and Tom enjoyed playing in. As the children are building in the sand, encourage them to retell that particular part of the story.

You could extend the talk for older or more able children by encouraging them to develop their own version of the story. What might happen to Tom and his speedboat? Does he decide to decorate it or watch in dismay as the donkeys trample over it? What adventures could he have if the speedboat suddenly roared into life?

land or picnic area which has hills and valleys. Let them explore and discuss the kinds of shapes they can make with dry sand.

As the children are modelling with their hands, talk to them about the actions they are using: pulling, shaping, holding the sand together, patting, etc. Ask them to describe what the sand feels like as they work with it: gritty, sharp, itchy, scratchy, cool.

Talk about how walls and hills hold their shapes. As the children use the pourers, ask them to describe the shape of the hills they have made: are they tall or low and spread out? Would it be hard work climbing them?

Follow-up
When the children have made their dry sand landscape, ask them to add their toys to promote imaginative talk.

Art and craft

Chapter six

Children need experience of a wide range of art and craft materials and techniques such as clay, play dough, junk modelling, printing and collage.

There are many ways of promoting different forms of talk within art and craft activities. Some of these centre on the medium used (chalk, pastel, crayon, felt-tipped pens and so on); some arise from the context of the task (making a play mat or a present for somebody special, for example). Others will depend on whether the children are working together to share their ideas.

Keep the emphasis on the speaking and listening, concentrating on the process rather than the end result. Try to involve even very young children in displaying their work from time to time.

Deciding on a display

Focus
Discussing how to set up a display table and helping children to make collective decisions.

What you need
A table or other display surface, a collection of objects related to the particular season of the year, for example, autumnal objects such as seeds, fruits, leaves; books, pictures, a large piece of suitably coloured fabric for a backdrop, containers.

Preparation
Discuss your starter collection of seasonal objects with the children (they can decide what they might add to this once the display is set up). During your discussion, draw their attention to the fact that the books and twigs are taller than the conkers and berries.
NB Warn the children about poisonous plants, fruits and seeds.

What to do
Tell the children that, between them, they are going to decide how best to arrange the collection so that all the objects can be seen and handled. For example, how would they like to use the fabric — as a backdrop or to cover the display surface? Which other things would look good hanging up? Do any of the objects such as rosehips or a twig with catkins need to go in water? Will they all be able to reach the prickly horse chestnuts without knocking the books over? How can they stop the conkers and berries from rolling away?

Hands on clay

Focus
Describing the qualities of clay through touch.

What you need
A fist-sized lump of clay for each child.

What to do
Give each child a lump of clay and let them simply play with it to begin with. This in itself is a good stimulus for talk because it builds on the children's natural inclination to explore the world through their senses. As they play, encourage the children to squeeze, pull, press and roll the clay. Extend their vocabulary by helping them to put a name to these actions. In the early stages, focus their talk on describing the texture of the clay. Does it feel soft, cold, slimy or dry? Does it feel the same all the way through or do the children notice that the texture changes as they work it? Can some of the children explain to others how they achieved particular effects such as a long, stretchy worm shape or a coil?

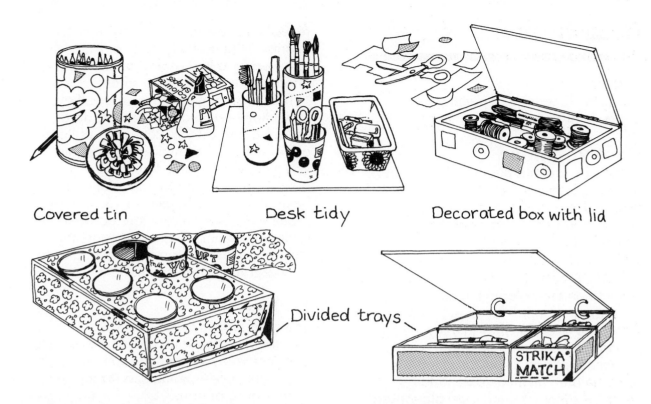

Covered tin Desk tidy Decorated box with lid

Divided trays

A special present

Focus
Thinking and talking about the likes and
dislikes of someone the children
know well.

What you need
Junk materials such as yoghurt pots,
cartons, tubes and boxes to use as
containers; catalogue pictures, fabric and
coloured paper for decoration; adhesive,
scissors.

Preparation
Talk to the children about some of the
containers they use regularly. Take the
marble box, for example. Why does it
have a lid? What reasons can the
children think of for having dividers in the
LEGO box? Tell the children they are
going to make a tidy or a storage
container as a present for a relative
or friend.

What to do
Discuss with the children who they would
like to make their tidy for and what that
person really enjoys doing. Ranjit, for
example, may tell you his sister is a keen
gardener, so perhaps a container to hold
packets of seeds would be a good
present for her. Talk about whether the
containers need lids or dividers and how
big they need to be.
   Ask the children how they could
decorate the containers, bearing in mind
their special person's favourite colours or
treasured possessions. They could try
using catalogue pictures or pieces of
fabric or paper to decorate in the
person's favourite colour.

Follow-up
Ask the children to cut out the pictures on
photocopiable page 95 and discuss the
people shown. Ask them which present
would be most useful for each person.
What else might the various characters
like and why?

Wrap it up

Focus
Putting the language of pattern, sequence and shape into context.

What you need
Sheets of wrapping paper with obvious repeating patterns, including some with pictures (for example, teddy bears or rockets) and others with geometric design.

What to do
Discuss with the children the pictures on the wrapping paper, focusing on colour, shape and size. Can they identify the big red circles, the small yellow squares or the star shapes on the wizard's hat? Some children might be able to talk about the different shades of colour used in the designs.

Encourage the children to examine and talk about the arrangement of patterns on the paper. Can the children describe how some go in lines across the paper while others run from top to bottom? Can they tell you about any repeating patterns? They may notice, for example, that there is a line of frogs followed by a line of dragonflies, then another line of frogs and so on.

Talk about any number groups they may identify such as two teddies, three kites and one ostrich. Repeating patterns are easier for the children to recognise if you talk the sequence through by pointing and saying together 'one big balloon, two small balloons' (or whatever sequence is obvious on your particular wrapping paper). This may enable the children to identify a rule for the pattern and to predict what comes next.

Follow-up
The children can make their own wrapping paper using one of the aspects of patterning you have talked about. Can they print in, for example, a straight line, or in groups of three? Give them a large and a small printer and let them make up their own pattern sequences.

Fantastic puppets

Focus
The language of fantasy and imagination.

What you need
Books such as David McKee's *Not Now, Bernard* (Andersen Press), June Counsel's *But Martin* (Corgi), Judith Kerr's *Mog in the Dark* (Picture Lions) and Jack Kent's *There's No Such Thing as a Dragon* (Blackie); comics, pictures, toys and wrapping paper which show a range of fantastical creatures.

Preparation
Help the children to recall and describe some of the fantastic creatures (dragons,

sock

card tubes or cones

card head taped to stick

pipe cleaner

stuffed sock or tights

sticks

monsters, robots, aliens, witches, wizards and so on) they may have seen in books, comics, pictures or on television.

Ask the children what it is about these creatures that makes them special. For example, the monster in *Not Now, Bernard* has a hairy, purple body, three toes on each paw, four sharp claws, pointed teeth, a long, red tongue, horns and a long nose. Discuss some of the amazing things that fantastic creatures can do that the children cannot (fly, cast spells, change shape at will).

Tell the children they are going to make some magic creatures of their own. Help them to decide how they will make them appear fantastic. Will their creatures have a long neck, wings, talons or giant-sized feet?

What to do

Ask the children to make their own imaginary characters in the form of simple puppets (see illustration). Help them to choose materials which highlight special features, for example, sequins or shiny buttons for eyes or soft fabric for floppy wings.

The children can use the puppets for imaginative play. What might the creatures say to each other if they met at a party?

Well done!

Focus

Different ways of praising each other.

What you need

Card or thick paper, crayons or felt-tipped pens.

What to do

Explain to the children that they are going to make badges to wear when they have done something praiseworthy. Help them to recall the special words you say to them when they have done something well. Talk about the catch-phrases other adults such as parents, grandparents or classroom helpers use when they praise the children: 'Well done!', 'Good work', 'You're a star', 'You've tried hard', 'Brilliant!'

Discuss the encouraging words children use to each other: 'I like your spaceship picture', 'Thank you for helping me.' Perhaps the children can teach each other how to say 'well done' in different languages. Can they tell you about some of the non-verbal ways of praising — smiles, hugs, a pat on the head? Talk about the signs, symbols and jingles computer programs offer as rewards for good effort.

Follow-up

Help the children to make some reward badges of their own. If they cannot manage the writing you could either act as a scribe or let them draw pictures.

Alternatively, you could put all their ideas on to a 'well done' poster and stick on a name label when a child has done something well.

Encourage the children to make badges or posters offering praise for good speaking and listening: 'I listened well', 'I took turns', 'I shared my ideas.'

Zoo play mat

Focus
Working with others, planning, listening and sharing ideas.

What you need
Toy zoo animals, pictures and books about zoos, thick card, a selection of boxes, tubes, cartons and other junk materials.

Preparation
Using the toy animals, books and pictures, discuss what the children already know about zoos. Name the animals and encourage the children who have visited a zoo to describe what they saw, while the others listen carefully. Tell the group they are going to work together to make a play mat.

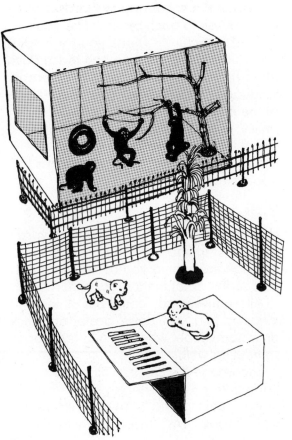

What to do
Encourage the children to share ideas about what they want to put on their play mat. Discuss which children might make different parts of the zoo. Younger children can plan and talk about fences and enclosures to stop the animals escaping. Can they decide what they might do about flying animals? What about lions and other dangerous animals? What else might animals need — trees, grazing, water? Older children could discuss what to do about pathways for people to move around comfortably, car parking, picnic areas and facilities for the disabled.

Feather prints

Focus
Through talk, helping children to see the link between cause and effect.

What you need
Feathers, paint-filled sponges (to make applying the paint to the feather easier), paper.

Preparation
Talk to the children about different ways of making marks on paper without using brushes. Can they remember what happened when they used their feet or hands, printed with cotton reels or made trails with sticks? Tell them that today they will be using feathers.

What to do
Give each child in the group a feather and show them how to load it using the paint-filled sponges (see illustration). Talk about the different hand movements the

children are using (flick, swirl, sweep, press, twist). Discuss the connections between these movements and the resulting marks on the paper. Can Rosie explain how she made her spotty print? What sort of marks did Jonathan make when he used his feather like a pencil? Ask Shiraz to describe and demonstrate how he made wavy lines.

Follow-up
● Use the same technique with other natural objects such as fir cones, stones or shells to help the children talk about the connection between cause and effect.
● The children could use natural objects to print more complex pictures.

Picture this

Focus
Close observation of illustrations to encourage children to develop their descriptive language.

What you need
A range of books showing different art techniques, for example, Wanda Gag's *Millions of Cats* (Puffin) — black-and-white pictures; Shigeo Watanabe's *How Do I Put It On?* (Puffin) — colouring in outline with pencil crayon; Joanne Oppenheim's *Have You Seen Birds?* (Hippo Books) — carefully crafted Plasticine pictures; *Necklace of Raindrops* or any other Joan Aiken stories — silhouettes; Ezra Keats's *Peter's Chair* (Red Fox) — collage. Books by Brian Wildsmith or Eric Carle show a range of wonderful techniques such as comb-scraping, rubbings, splash-painting and finger-painting. You will also need art materials suitable for the chosen technique.

Preparation

Tell the children they are going to look closely at some pictures in story-books. Ask them to describe the illustrations in a range of books. Help them to identify the different techniques used to make the pictures (chalk, pastel, comb-scraping, etc.). Eric Carle's *The Very Quiet Cricket* (Hamish Hamilton), for example, provides you with an opportunity to talk about how the lacy wings on the locust, bee, and dragonfly have been made by rubbings and the green and red apples on the tree are finger-painted; Brian Wildsmith's *Fishes* (Oxford University Press) shows different ways of creating watery effects.

What to do

Choose one of the books from your collection and tell the children they are going to look very carefully at the pictures so that they can make their own in the same way.

Talk to the children about some of the materials used to get particular effects. How has the doily been used in *Peter's Chair*? What might the children use a doily for in their own pictures (lacy effects, flowers, raised surfaces, etc.)? Would newsprint, wallpaper and magazine pictures be useful?

Let the children create their own collages — or whatever technique you have chosen — to illustrate the story in the book, or any other story or topic they like.

Paintspa

Focus
Using a computer art program to help the children talk about cause and effect, and decision making.

What you need
A computer program such as *Paintspa* (Nimbus) or *First Paint* (Archimedes).

Preparation
Using programs such as these, the children can draw and 'paint' on the screen, choosing their colours and using the mouse to move the 'brush'. Allow time for the children to become used to the link between moving the mouse and the marks made on the screen.

What to do
As they create their pictures, talk with the children about the decisions they are making. Ask questions like: what colour do you need for the basket? Will white paint show up on the white screen? Is the face outline large enough to draw in the eyes, nose and mouth? Talk about the thickness of the brush line and whether selecting a thinner one would help to paint in the windows, etc.

Explore the spray, splatter, blob and fan brush effects, and discuss how these could help with the children's picture making. Would any of these effects be useful for a giant's beard, for example? Do the blow prints remind the children of anything? Can they see any pictures in the fan shape which they might be able to incorporate into their own pictures?

Mood music

Focus
Listening carefully and responding to the mood of music.

What you need
A short piece of music which evokes an obvious mood or movement such as Tchaikovsky's *Nutcracker Suite* ('Dance of the reeds', 'Chinese Dance', 'Russian dance'), or try some of the children's favourite TV and film themes. You will also need paint and paintbrushes, wax crayons, chalk, pastels and plain paper.

Preparation
Prepare the children for listening to the music by explaining that music gives messages, just as talking does. Listen to a short extract of music and talk about its mood and movement: strong, gentle, shivery or explosive.

What to do
Play the music a second time. Ask the children to move their hands with the music and help them to describe what they are doing. Tchaikovsky's 'Dance of the reeds' and 'The Chinese dance', will encourage tiny light dabs and points with the fingers, with some floating curls and swirls. 'The Russian dance', from the same ballet, suggests spiky, jerky movements, and quick opening and closing of the fingers.

Talk about what the hand movements might look like as patterns and lines on paper: straight, jagged, broken, smooth, curved, spiral, tiny spots and dabs.

Play the music as the children draw or paint their ideas of the music's mood.

Discovery area

Chapter seven

Very often in early years classrooms the discovery area will be a display or interest table, for the children to have hands-on experience of a stimulating collection of materials. Of course, it could be a corner where you set up a finding-out activity for the day. It is often a good idea to let the children explore the materials on their own or talk among themselves about the objects on display.

   You could do one of the suggested activities with a large group and then leave the materials for the children to work with independently afterwards. Or you might like to gradually incorporate some of the follow-up activities and use them as part of a topic.

Minibeasts

Focus
Descriptive language through close observation of minibeasts.

What you need
A collection of minibeasts (this will depend on the time of year and availability) and their natural habitats, for example, tree and leaf litter or pond water, in suitable containers; magnifiers, handling equipment (twigs, spoons and lids), high-quality pictures and line drawings of minibeasts, information and fiction books.

Preparation
Temper the children's natural enthusiasm for picking things up without thinking by pointing out sensitively that some creatures, such as those that live in the water, will not survive if taken out of their natural surroundings or handled too much. Others may sting or bite. Explain to the children that all living things need space in which to move about, air, food and water.

NB Make sure the children wash their hands after handling minibeasts and check that none of the children has an allergic reaction to insect stings.

What to do
Observe and discuss your particular collection of minibeasts with the children. Talk about their size, colours and patterns. Is the creature a fast mover like the spider or a slow one like the snail? Ask the children to consider the connection between the number of legs and speed of movement. Do the creatures jump, swim, glide, crawl or scurry? Do they have wings and are they easy to see?

Talk about whether all the creatures have a head and a body and how many segments the children can see. What sort of textures do the creatures' bodies have? Encourage descriptive words such as a protective shell, shiny, soft and furry.

Ask the children to compare and contrast each minibeast's eyes with their own. How many has it got and where are they?

If the creatures are safe to handle, invite the children to place them on their hands and describe what it feels like. Does it tickle, feel slimy, cold or smooth? Did the children expect it to feel like that or were they surprised?

Follow-up
• Using photocopiable page 96, tell the children to look closely at the minibeast on the leaf and ask them how many more they can find just like it. Talk about similarities and differences in shape, size, number of legs and wings, etc.
• Look for and talk about some of the clues minibeasts leave which give us more information about them, such as chewed leaves, snail trails, caterpillar droppings and worm casts.
• Can the children work out what their live creatures might be by matching them to the labelled pictures and line drawings on display? Encourage them to use language such as: it has six legs, wings and a body, it must be . . . which helps with classifying and sorting activities.

• Ask the children to make a simple model or line drawing based on their discussions and observations.
• Look at minibeasts in story-books and discuss how close these are to the real thing. Stimulating examples can be found in Eric Carle's *The Very Busy Spider* (Hamish Hamilton) and *The Very Hungry Caterpillar* (Puffin), Babette Cole's *The Slimy Book* (Picture Lions) and Allan and Janet Ahlberg's *Worm Book* (Picture Lions).

Growth

Focus
Identifying and talking about the elements needed for growing plants by looking at bulbs, soils and containers.

What you need
Bulbs; containers from the junk box; two contrasting types of soil, for example, clay, loam, sandy or chalky (if you use soil from the garden you are likely to get a natural variation); sieves, white paper, a knife, magnifying glasses.

What to do
Tell the children to look closely at, and discuss the bulb. Ask them if they have seen something like it before — an onion, perhaps. Discuss the shape of the bulb and the fact that it has two ends: the tip and the fibrous roots. Ask the children to describe the colour: is it the same all over or are there different shades? Now invite them to smell it. Does it remind them of anything? Describe what the bulb feels like, focusing on words such as silky, smooth and papery.

Invite the children to speculate about what might be inside the bulb and make suggestions for finding out. For example,

they might consider peeling it, cutting it up or pulling it apart. Open the bulb up and ask the children to describe what they see and feel. Is the flesh the same all the way through? What patterns can the children identify, and which way do the lines and circles go? Let them trace these with their fingers, then use magnifiers to take a closer look.

NB Make sure the children wash their hands afterwards.

Explore and discuss two types of soil. Talk about one type at a time. Give each child in the group some soil and a piece of white paper. Ask the children to talk about what they expect to see. Tip some soil on to the paper and discuss the colours: can the children see different shades of brown and yellow or detect any white flecks? Allow the children to explore the texture with their hands and describe what it feels like: rough, smooth, sharp, gritty and so on. What else can the children identify in their soil and describe to others — sticks, roots, pebbles? Ask them to use magnifiers and sieves to

locate other soil elements they may not have noticed before.

The children should do the same with the second type of soil, then discuss the similarities and differences between the two.

Follow-up
● Plant some bulbs with the whole group, using their suggestions about what you will need and how to go about it. Discuss, for instance, which way round the children think the bulbs should be planted and how far down they need to be. Do they think the bulbs would be happiest outside or indoors? You could try out some of their suggestions in different pots and discuss what happens at regular intervals.
● Ask a small group to choose containers from the junk box and to plant some class bulbs. Allow them to make their own decisions about which containers to use, but encourage them to justify their choices. Over time, discuss the effectiveness of the containers: are some too shallow or let all the compost through? What has happened to the cardboard containers?

Ourselves

Focus
Helping children to recall and recount incidents from their personal history.

What you need
Group or individual photographs, or children's drawings of themselves.

What to do
The children are going to recount an incident from their personal history to others in the group. This could be an adventure or a mishap, or the time they said or did something which made everybody laugh.

Tell the children to ask their parents about a memorable incident, losing Dad in the supermarket or getting the potty stuck on their head, for instance. In school, ask the children to share these examples from their personal history by retelling the story. Encourage them to bring in the pictures or photographs of themselves. These could either show the child alone or as part of a group. They need not relate directly to the incident, as long as the children can say things like: 'This is me when I was two', 'This is me with my friends.'

The children might like to invite their parents in to give their version of the same story or share their own memories of when they were younger.

Follow-up
● Look at some of the group photographs or drawings and ask the children to pick out people other than themselves to talk about. Concentrate on the words or phrases frequently used by that person, for example, 'My Mum always calls me poppet' or 'My baby brother says "more, more!".' You could record some of these words and phrases and ask the children to match the voices to the pictures of the child talking.
● Look at some of the faces in the photographs with the children and discuss the emotions portrayed: happy, bored, worried, puzzled, etc.
● Make an 'Ourselves' tape for others to listen to and have fun with. The recordings could include languages we know, wishes, dreams, messages and jokes.

Story Corner

Focus
Talking and listening using story-books as a stimulus.

What you need
A collection of story-books, including a range of pictures and minimal-text books. Use whatever you already have or try some of these authors: Jan Ormerod, Shirley Hughes, Sarah Garland, Ron Maris, John Prater, Raymond Briggs and Philippe Dupasquier; either your own or commercially produced story tapes such as Shirley Hughes's Alfie stories or Mairi Hedderwick's Katie Morag stories. You will also need a cassette player, finger puppets, hats and a flannel board.

What to do
Let the children select a favourite picture book from your collection. Ask them to retell it with a friend, putting their own words to the pictures. Before they begin, recap on the major events of the story by helping the children to 'read' the pictures.

The children might enjoy making up names for the characters and giving them different voices. What sounds might the baby make? What might the shopkeeper be saying to the little girl? As the children become more confident with this approach, ask them to look more closely at the illustrations for clues to embellish the story: what expressions do the characters have on their faces? What else can the children deduce about characters and actions by looking closely at the different settings?

Follow-up
● Play the children an extract from a story tape and ask them to identify which story it comes from. Cue them into listening for the clues they get from

names, refrains and descriptions of surroundings.

Fruits

Focus
Descriptive language which comes from exploring fruit.

What you need
A collection of fruits which give a variety of shapes, colours, sizes and textures, a knife, paper plates or squares of kitchen towel.

What to do
Wash the fruit and tell the children not to taste it without checking with an adult first.

Pass the fruit around and ask the children to describe what it looks, feels and smells like. What shapes and colours can they name? Does it feel soft and squidgy or hard and furry? Do the fruits have a sharp, tangy smell or perhaps one the children do not like? Ask them to predict what they think they are going to find inside.

Open the fruit up and talk about any new colours and shapes the children can now see. How do these compare with the outside skin? Discuss the number and arrangement of seeds and pips. Pick up on any surprises the children may notice. Did they expect to see so many pips in an apple, for example, or did they think they might be black rather than white? There may even be bugs to discuss! The children may be surprised that the flesh of certain oranges is red, while others have no seeds at all. The kiwi and ugli fruits are useful examples to use for contrasting outer and inner appearance and textures.

Follow-up
● Play a game of 'Guess the fruit'. Let the children take turns to choose a fruit without the other players seeing, and then describe the size, texture, colour and shape. Can other children guess which fruit it is?

● Use words which describe the texture of the fruits to sort and classify: hard, smooth, furry, squidgy. Try building on this language in a creative way: 'it feels as bristly as my granddad's chin', 'as smooth as my mum's knee' or 'as tickly as a spider crawling up my arm.'

● Ask the children to close their eyes. Let them smell, then taste a small piece of fruit. Check that none of the children is allergic to the fruits first. Can they identify it? Ask the children to give reasons for their guesses by using taste and smell words, for instance, 'I think it's a grapefruit because it's sharp and makes my nose all tingly.'

Music-makers

Focus
Listening to and discriminating between different sounds, and building up a vocabulary to describe them.

What you need
Everyday materials for making sounds such as paper, a yoghurt pot, a metal teapot, a tube, a whistle, an elastic band, a bell, sandpaper, beaters (a wooden spoon, a ruler, a pencil, a straw); or musical instruments such as: woodblocks, a drum, coconut shells, shakers, bells, a tambourine, a recorder, a cymbal, beaters with hard and soft heads.

What to do
Let the children experiment with the collection of sound-makers, allowing them lots of time to practise and repeat the activities. Discuss the variety of sounds produced when the children try out different ways of playing the instruments: tap, flick, shake, blow. Can the children make sounds with all the instruments if they play them in these ways?

Help the children sort the instruments into the following sets: how they can be played (shake, scrape, blow, tap); the kinds of sounds they make (high/low or long/short), sounds we like/don't like; and materials used to make them (wood, plastic, metal).

Follow-up
• Ask the children to play the following game: working with a partner, the children face each other with two instruments in between them. Child A shuts his eyes or goes behind a screen, while child B plays one of the instruments. Child A opens his eyes and tries to guess which instrument his partner has just played.
• Ask the children to play the following game working in pairs. Give each child one instrument. Child A plays a single sound in a particular way, for example, a short, sharp tap or a loud, ringing sound. Child B has to copy the sound as closely as possible, like an echo. After some practice, encourage the children to make patterns of sounds such as: getting louder or softer, quickening up or slowing down.

69

Pets' corner

Focus
Talking about pets.

What you need
A pet brought in specially for the day.

Preparation
Talk to the children about all the necessary arrangements for bringing the pet to school: asking their parents for permission, getting it to school safely, toilet and exercise arrangements. Can the children all bring their pets in at the same time or would it be better to take turns? Discuss what the animal will need to eat and drink during the day and how the children should behave near it. Will it get frightened easily? What sort of voices should the children use when approaching the animal?

What to do
Ask the children to listen carefully to the pet's owner while he or she tells them about the animal. What is its name and why is it called that? Can the owner recall and describe any funny adventures or times when the pet has been a comfort?

Encourage the rest of the group to ask the owner questions which help them to find out about the animal's diet, sleep patterns and how much exercise it needs.

Follow-up
● Talk about what would happen if the family went away on holiday and somebody else had to look after the pet. Can the children devise simple instructions that would tell others how to look after it? You could keep this as a purely verbal exercise or put the instructions into picture form.
● By encouraging the children to observe the pet closely during the day and asking the owner questions, discuss how the animal communicates. How can you tell when it is happy, sad or afraid? How does it let you know when it is hungry or wants to go to the toilet? Does it dream? Talk about some of the warning signals it uses when strangers or other animals approach it.

Ask these children to tell you about their pets.

Salid
Paloma
Robert
Ben
Sania

Listen to the story.

Simone brought in her rabbit. She told us Snowy needs:
Shelter
Food
Drink
space

Make the animal noise

Hall or big space

Chapter eight

In this chapter, you will find activities which require more space as they involve movement, some large apparatus or large group games. You can use any decent-sized space you have, either inside or outside the building, as long as it is free of obstacles.

   Use the opportunities which such a space provides to encourage the children to listen, since this is as important as the moving about.

Anansi

Focus
Reciting a rhyme and listening carefully for cues.

What you need
No special requirements.

What to do
Teach the children the rhyme below.

Anansi, Anansi, spider man,
Catch me, catch me if you can.

Choose one child to be Anansi and ask him or her to turn away from the rest of the players in the game. The group chants the above rhyme, adding a final line: 'What are you doing, Anansi?' On hearing this last line, Anansi turns round to face the other players, who must stand still and listen very carefully to the response. Anansi might say, 'Eating my dinner', 'lazing by the river', 'climbing a tree', etc. Anansi turns away again and the rest of the players repeat the rhyme. When Anansi replies, 'Playing tricks!', all the other children must run to a home base to avoid being caught. The first child to be caught in the chase becomes the next Anansi. If nobody is caught, Anansi returns to the front.

This is the way

Focus
Adapting a rhyme, listening to movement words and translating them into actions.

What you need
No special requirements.

Preparation
Familiarise the children with the song 'Here we go round the mulberry bush' and practise the actions.

What to do
Using the tune of 'Here we go round the mulberry bush', adapt the rhyme to incorporate large body movements. Teach the children some examples: leap up high, swing our legs/arms and turn around. Can the children think of any more movements to sing and try out? Ask them to demonstrate their suggestions to the others in the group: curl up small, bend our knees, jump like frogs and so on.

Follow-up
Try putting other words to the 'Mulberry bush' song or use the same technique with different songs such as 'If you're happy and you know it' or 'Aiken Drum'.

Explain to the children that when you give the signal to start, they have to move on, over and through 'the rainforest' as if the animals were playing happily. The children must listen very carefully as they move around because when you say 'Snap!', they must curl up small on the floor and be as still as possible, to avoid being gobbled up by the crocodile. They can move again only when you give the release command 'Croc's gone!'.

When the children are familiar with the game, instead of asking them to move freely over the apparatus, give them more specific movements to do before the 'Snap!' command, for example, crawling, sliding, pulling themselves along the floor or making star shapes.

Robots

Focus
Giving and receiving instructions, and introducing children to the language used for robotic toy commands.

What you need
A bean bag or other small object.

What to do
Put the children into pairs. One child is going to pretend to be a robot and the other its operator. Tell the children that the robot has to do exactly what the operator says. This means the robot has to listen very carefully while the programmer tries to give very clear instructions.

The instructions must be verbal only — no pointing, pushing or touching. Let the children practise the four basic commands used to direct robotic toys: forwards, backwards, left and right. How will the robot know when to stop? When

Croc's gone

Focus
Listening for keywords and following instructions.

What you need
Any large apparatus you have available such as benches, stools, barrels and mats.

What to do
Tell the children to imagine the apparatus you have put out is a rainforest and to pretend to be some of the forest creatures. Warn them there is a hungry crocodile on the loose waiting for its supper.

the children are more practised at giving and receiving instructions in this way, introduce them to the idea of moving in a measured number of paces ('units'). Ask the 'operator' to direct the 'robot' to a specific location (a bean bag or other small object). Help the children to identify invalid commands such as 'three more' or 'over here near the door'.

Get round it

Focus
Giving and receiving instructions.

What you need
Large toys such as dumper trucks, tricycles or scooters, skittles, mats, cardboard boxes, bean bags and hoops.

What to do
Set up an obstacle course with the skittles and boxes (or anything else you have which suits the purpose). Direct the children on their large toys around the course. Tell them they will have to listen very carefully to your instructions.

To begin with, space the obstacles out in a straight line. Talk the children through the course giving instructions such as 'around the box', 'in between the skittles', 'in front of the hoops'. When the children have more experience of following these kinds of directions, set out the course more randomly. Instruct the children to go between the two yellow skittles, around the red hoop and so on.

Follow-up
● As they become more competent, let the children try this activity in pairs, with one child driving, the other directing.

Come over here!

Focus
Developing listening skills, co-operation and mathematical vocabulary.

What you need
Enough hoops for half the group size, a whistle or a tambourine.

What to do
Place the hoops on the floor around the room. Tell the children that on the start signal (blow the whistle or bang the tambourine) they must run, skip or jump around the room, but they are not allowed in the hoops.

They must listen carefully for the stop signal and the instructions which will follow. Give instructions based on number language, for instance, 'Make groups of three in the hoops.' Encourage the children to co-operate by calling for

Miming messages

someone to join them if there are too few in their hoop, or by showing others where there is a space if they have already formed a set of three. Tell them to try not to leave anybody out.

If there are remainders, discuss with the children why this is so (the class may not be divisible by three). With more able or older children, try instructing them to have 'no more' than three, four or five in their hoop.

Follow-up
Try playing a similar game but without the hoops. Tell the children to jump around until they hear the stop signal. This time, give instructions about numbers and actions, for instance, two to make a bridge, three to make a web, five to make a wriggly monster.

Focus
Helping children to be aware of, and interpret, body language as an important aspect of speaking and listening.

What you need
No special requirements.

What to do
Warn the children that you will not be talking for a while, and that they must watch you very carefully to know what to do. Now ask them to carry out your instructions using only mime such as this one: 'All of you [make sweeping gestures] look [point at your eyes] at me [point to yourself].' Make sure the children have understood the mime and repeat it if necessary.

Try other silent instructions: 'All of you [sweeping gesture] stand up [palms upwards].' Wait until the children have all stood up, then gesture 'thank you' (smile or thumbs up). Get the children to sit down (palms to the floor).

When the children's attention is focused on you, talk about how they understood your gestures. Ask them to recall and demonstrate any gestures they use, or other people use to them, for instance, stop, come here, turn around. Can the rest of the group follow the instructions?

Follow-up
Draw out signs and gestures that are especially helpful for speaking and listening such as smiles and nods, 'I don't understand' or 'I don't agree.'

Listen to the beat

Focus
Memorising and linking a sound signal with a movement, and discrimination of sounds.

What you need
Instruments to give sound signals to children, for example, a drum, a tambourine, a tambour.

Preparation
Remind the children how to listen for 'stop' and 'start' signals by playing a simple game of musical statues. For example, shake the tambourine as a signal to start moving and bang the tambour as a signal to stand still.

What to do
This time, tell the children that on the signal (a shake of the tambourine) they are going to walk in any direction they like around the room. When they hear quick taps on the tambourine this means they are going to change direction. Keep the same stop signal (a single bang on the tambourine).

Practise this until the children are confident about listening and responding appropriately to the signals. Reinforce the activity changing the movements you ask the children to make: from walking on their toes, change to walking on their heels; from walking with feet wide apart, change to walking with feet close together.

Follow-up
Play a tambourine in different ways to represent various movements. Can the children discriminate between a walk (slow, regular beats) and a skip (tum te tum rhythm), a run (quick, even beats) and a stop signal (bang)?

Buzz

Focus
Listening carefully to discriminate a particular sound from a background buzz, just as children have to focus their attention in class.

What you need
No special requirements.

What to do
Divide the children into two groups called Mangoes and Pears. Check that they all understand which group they are in. Explain that on a given signal they are going to walk around the room saying their group name all the time. Tell the children they must say nothing else at all. When they meet up with somebody else saying the name of the same fruit, they should join hands. They must keep going until they find everybody in their group.

There will almost certainly be at least two or three chains of both Mangoes and Pears going around at the same time. Chains belonging to the same fruit name should join up.

Follow-up
• Increase the number of groups by adding other fruits.
• Change the buzzwords to fit a theme you may be concentrating on in class.
• Change the words to make different animal sounds.

blue team

Noughts and crosses

Focus
Mathematical vocabulary, giving and receiving instructions leading up to strategic play.

What you need
Markers such as bean bags, mats or hoops; four yellow and four blue bands.

What to do
Play a game of noughts and crosses with the children as counters. Lay out a three-by-three grid using bean bags or hoops as markers, or chalk lines on the ground if you are playing outside (see illustration). Familiarise the children with the grid using terms such as top, bottom, middle, rows, columns, left and right.

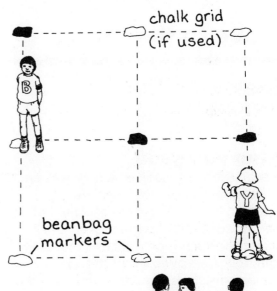

chalk grid (if used)

beanbag markers

children as 'counters'

yellow team

Divide the children into two teams, one yellow and one blue. Choose four children from each team to be the counters (noughts and crosses). Ask them to wear a coloured band. The other members of the team instruct each of the 'counters' in turn to stand on the grid until they have three in a row or column. Encourage the children to use terms which help to place the counters in the correct position: in between, left-hand corner, bottom row, etc.

Follow-up
● Make the game more difficult by asking the children to spot the diagonals to score a winning row.
● Change the shape and size of the grid, and ask the children to aim for four in a row.

Move to the music

Focus
Listening and responding to a feeling of movement in music.

What you need
A short piece of music which evokes an obvious quality of movement, for instance, Rimsky-Korsakov's 'Dance of the buffoons' (quick, light movements); Borodin's 'Polovtsian dances' (slow and light, followed by fast and strong movements); Saint-Saëns' *Carnival of the Animals*; film and TV theme music.

Preparation
Prepare the children for listening to the music by explaining that music 'moves' just as we can move with our bodies. It might move gently, slowly, softly, quickly, lightly.

What to do
Ask the children to sit and listen to a short piece of music. Share ideas about the quality of its movement. For example, Rimsky-Korsakov's 'Dance of the buffoons' is very exciting — it moves quickly and lightly, evoking running and scurrying movements.

Play the music a second time and encourage the children to move freely as the music tells them to. As they dance, look for any fast movements, flicks and darts the children make. Stop the music again and ask some of the children to demonstrate what they have been doing. Talk about how their movements match the movement of the music.

Outside the room

Chapter nine

This chapter offers some suggestions for extending the children's speaking and listening activities beyond the immediate room in which you usually work. You will be developing different forms of talk when you take the children around the rest of the building, around the locality, encourage links with parents, carers and community members or make trips to places of interest. These are perfect opportunities to encourage the children to take note and talk about some of the things they may have taken for granted or never thought about before.

Do not forget to find out how many adults are legally required to accompany your group, get permission from parents and inform people where you are going.

What can we hear?

Focus
Helping children to identify, describe and recall sounds.

What you need
No special requirements.

Preparation
Take the children into the playground, the playing fields or a local street for a 'sound walk'. Just before you go out, ask them to sit quietly and concentrate on the sounds they can hear. Can the children locate and identify doors banging, children's voices in other parts of the building or toilets flushing, for example?

What to do
Take the children outside. Ask them to stand quietly and to listen very carefully for any sounds they can hear. After a short time, ask the children to tell the others what they have heard. Someone might say she heard 'squeak, squeak'. Ask the other children if they can hear it, too.

To help them discriminate the squeak from other sounds, talk about whether it is near or far away, and if it goes on all the time or stops and starts. Once most of the children can tune into the sound, ask them if they can suggest what might be making it. What other things do they know that squeak like that? If the response is 'mouse', accept it as a good idea, but ask if it is likely or possible. Would a mouse make a noise as loud as that?

As children offer suggestions for other sounds they can hear, see if they can begin to put them into groups: people sounds (laughter, footsteps, coughing), information sounds (car horns, the clink of milk bottles, ringing telephones), mechanical sounds (lawn-mowers, concrete mixers, chainsaws), animal sounds (dogs barking, horses trotting by, cats miaowing), musical sounds (singing, whistling, someone playing the piano).

Which sounds are near and which are far away? Ask the children to listen for high and low sounds and those which are either pleasant or unpleasant. Help them to describe the sounds they hear: screech, hiss, roar, rumble, scrape, buzz and so on. Encourage the children to practise making the sounds with their voices.

Follow-up
• When you return to the classroom, you could extend the idea of classifying and recalling sounds by making a simple chart to display. Discuss which of the sounds you have heard could fit into more than one group.
• Ask the children to make a picture book of sounds they like and those they do not like.
• Ask them to compare the sounds they heard inside and outside the room. How were they different? Were there any sounds they only heard in one place?

Our favourites

Focus
Listening to and talking about anecdotes, favourite tales and rhymes.

What you need
A tape recorder and blank tapes.

Preparation
Make a bank of other people's favourite stories and rhymes and the anecdotes associated with them. The most effective way of doing this is to record them on tape. But if this is not possible, you could consider asking people in to talk to the children or put the stories into a simple book to share. You do not need to make a huge collection or compile it all in one go. You could build it up gradually or change the content regularly: who is on the tape today?

Introduce the session to the children by recounting your own favourite rhyme, song or tale, and explaining why it is special to you. Perhaps it is a bedtime story your grandma read to you when you were a child. Or a song playing on the radio when you were decorating and put your foot in the bucket. Ask the children if they have favourites, too, and why some rhymes or stories are special for them.

What to do
Discuss with the children who they would like to invite in to share their stories: the secretary, other teachers or helpers, other children, the cook or cleaner, perhaps. Make sure you check with them first — it may not be convenient.

If it helps with organisation, you could encourage the children to take turns to take a tape home and ask their parents and other community members to make a recording. Making such tapes means that the children will experience a wide range of voices — young and old, male and female, with different accents and dialects.

Good times, bad times

Focus
Exploring feelings about the playground and talking about appropriate behaviour.

What you need
No special requirements.

Preparation
Talk to the children about what happens in the playground – how they can make the most of what they enjoy and how any difficulties or worries could be resolved.

Using your playground duty or supervision time to observe your children playing is a useful way into a follow-up discussion.

What to do
On a warm day, observe your children at play. When it is time to go back inside, keep your group outside for a short time to talk about what they have been doing. If you prefer to take the children inside, make sure the discussion takes place immediately, so that the children have instant recall.

Ask the children to tell you what they have enjoyed during playtime. Perhaps they relish the different opportunities it gives them, such as playing with friends in different classes, meeting up with brothers and sisters, access to the climbing frames and large toys, being in a big, open space or chatting to teachers. Use your observations to praise them first for all the good things you saw them doing and give them examples: 'It was good to see Farrukh and Anna taking turns'; 'Dejay was very kind to Charlie when he fell over'; 'Thank you for putting your litter in the bin.'

Ask the children to think of reasons why it is better not to play ball games in certain areas of the playground and why there may be quiet areas or no-go zones.

Inevitably, you will have seen examples of misbehaviour, too – pushing, teasing or excluding others from games. Discuss other issues which worry the children about playtime. How does it make them feel when unpleasant things happen to them? How can we help others who are upset?

Ask the children if they have any suggestions for resolving some of these difficult situations. How about asking politely or listening when somebody says she does not like being chased with a plastic spider? When is it a good idea to ask an adult for help?

It is important to encourage children to express how they feel about things on a regular basis. Discuss issues as they arise and help them to find positive ways forward.

Headteacher
Mrs M. O'Neal

A taped tour

Focus
Taping a running commentary around the building.

What you need
A tape recorder and a blank tape.

Preparation
You are going to make a running commentary with a small group of children as you tour the building. Before you begin, make sure you warn other people in the building who may be working, too.

Explain to the children they are going on a tour, so they can learn where everything is and who works in the different areas. Explain that this will enable them to find their way around when they need to go to special places: getting a book from the library, taking a message to the secretary or having lunch in the dining room. They will also be able to show visitors and new children around when they arrive. Make sure the children understand that you will be stopping in lots of different places and describing what you see and hear.

What to do
When you arrive at the first area for discussion, before you record, ask the children to identify where they are, for example, 'we're outside the caretaker's office.' Then start the tape and say where you are. Stop the tape. Talk about what you see there: the colour of the door, labels, equipment, shelves and so on. Start the tape and record your description. Stop the tape. Are there any noises the children would like to record that are characteristic of the area: typewriters, telephones ringing, kitchen-equipment noises or clanging buckets? Agree on what you want to record. Start the tape and record your choice. Stop the tape. Discuss with the children what you have seen. What are these things used for and who uses them? Are the people you have seen always there? Record some of these discussion points. Stop the tape.

Follow this procedure for each area you visit on your tour.

Follow-up
When you get back to your own room, play the tape. Leave out the first sentence that says where you are. Then ask the children to listen very carefully. Can they deduce which area is being described in that part of the commentary?

Other people's jobs

Focus
Talking about how to find out more about somebody's job.

What you need
A friendly person who will allow you to look around his or her workplace. The following activity is about a discussion after a visit to the school cook, but the talking points are easily adapted to link in with any other visit you may choose to make.

Preparation
Arrange your visit beforehand and agree on how many children can be conveniently and safely accommodated. Before you go on the visit, encourage the children to speculate about the cook's job and the kinds of things that happen in the kitchen.

What to do
Following your visit to the cook, talk to the children about what they have seen. This will help to confirm any ideas they had about the job, correct misinformation and show them what else they want to find out.

Talk about any tins and packets the children spotted in the kitchen. Were the labels the same as those they have seen at home? Help them to recall sizes and ask if they have seen any as big as that in the supermarket. Where might the cook buy them?

Discuss other people the children saw and what they were doing (making pastry, grating cheese, etc.). Ask them if they think the same people do those jobs all the time. What sorts of equipment, such as buckets and mops, can the children remember seeing? Talk about whose job it might be to use some of these things.

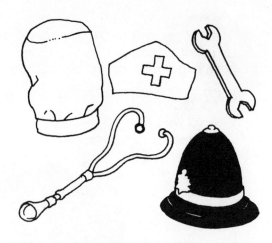

Now ask the children to consider the cook herself. What was she wearing and why? How does she know what to cook? Discuss what else her job might entail.

Follow-up
After your discussion, you could suggest that the children invite the cook in to talk about some of the things they still want to find out. Help them to think of the questions they would like to ask her. Rehearse fair, sensible and polite ways of finding out what they want to know.

Talk walk

Focus
Helping children to be aware of different forms of talk and how people use their voices.

What you need
A camera, paper, clipboards, pencils, a tape recorder.

Preparation
You are going to be taking a group of children to your local shopping centre or main street, where you will hear a range of spoken languages. Before you go, talk

to the children about what they have used their own voices for so far that day: asking for and offering help, explaining something, arguing, chatting and so on.

What to do

Have a word with the children about road safety and the importance of staying together. While you are out with the children, stop at strategic points where you see or hear something happening, and ask the children to listen carefully. Talk about what they hear. For example, at the bus stop, there may be people asking about the time of the next bus, buying a ticket or having a chat. Help the children to identify these different forms of talk.

Move on to another area. What is the stall-holder or news vendor shouting, for instance? Can the children understand the words? Have they heard shouts like this anywhere else? Outside the shop or supermarket, ask the children to listen out for laughter, complaining or angry voices.

Have the children noticed that they have heard a range of languages and voices: young and old, male and female, accents and dialects? Which dialect words are the children familiar with and can they explain what they mean?

As you walk around, point out evidence of different languages and alphabets on shop fronts, restaurants, travel agencies or cinemas. Can anyone say these aloud? If not, take a picture or copy it down and ask someone to translate later.

Follow-up

When you get back, discuss with the children what they have heard on the walk. Give them reminders such as 'Remember when we were outside the fish-and-chip shop . . .' You could encourage the children to act out some of the events they saw. Can they make their voices sound like the news vendor or chat like the people waiting for the bus?

We're off!

Focus

Involving children in talking about the preparations for a visit.

What you need

Fiction and information books.

What to do

The following activity outlines the talk which could arise from involving the children in preparations for a visit to a farm park. It can be easily adapted to link in to any other visit you choose to make.

Using books, pictures and toy animals as a starting point, discuss what sorts of

animals the children think they might see when they get to the farm park. Encourage any children who have visited one before or who have friends or relatives working there to recall and recount their experiences, while others listen carefully.

Have a word about safety and behaviour towards the animals. What reasons can the children think of for having fences and special places to feed the animals? Talk about practical considerations such as clothing, and the sort of food and drink to take with them. Ask the children to consider if it is likely to be hot, cold or wet and suggest appropriate clothing and footwear. What else do the children think they should bring with them?

Is there anybody in the group with special needs, such as mobility difficulties, fear of animals or a special diet? Encourage the children to make their own suggestions about trying to make everybody comfortable and happy.

Round the block

Focus
Talking about the built environment.

What you need
Clipboards, paper, pencils, a camera.

Preparation
Help the children to remember and talk about the buildings and special places they see on the way to school each day. Does anybody pass the library, the post office or the newsagent's, for example?

Tell the children you are going to take them on a short walk around the block to have a careful look around.

What to do
On your walk, you may pass some of the children's own houses or those belonging to friends and relatives. Discuss these and any other personal landmarks such as the low wall they always walk on or the junction where the crossing patrol person helps them to cross the road. It is a good idea to take some photographs or make simple sketches as visual reminders for the follow-up activities.

Draw the children's attention to, and discuss, other buildings such as the post office, the library or the swimming pool. Ask them questions such as 'what happens in here?', 'Who uses this building?', 'Why is it in this particular place do you think?', 'Do you have to pay to go in?'

Talk about any road markings and signposts you see along the way. What do they tell us? Ask the children to think of reasons why these are in that particular location. Point out and discuss some of the smaller objects you pass, for example, litter bins and post-boxes. Are there any benches for people to sit and rest? How many notice-boards and advertising hoardings can they spot?

Follow-up

Help the children to recreate the walk by making a simple picture map using photographs or drawings.

Doors on history

Focus

Introducing children to the language associated with historical investigations.

What you need

Clipboards, paper, pencils, a camera.

Preparation

You are going to be taking the children out on a walk to look at and talk about doors as clues to history. Prepare them for the walk by considering the doors they see in school. Discuss why there are some double doors or why others may have wire mesh on them. Familiarise the children with the vocabulary of doors —

frames, hinges, knobs, knockers, handles, panels, panes and locks.

What to do

On your walk, draw the children's attention to the many different types of doors in evidence all around them by asking questions such as these: 'What kinds of buildings have doors?', 'Why do some need double doors?', 'Why do others shut automatically or fold up like a concertina?' Ask them to speculate about where closed doors might lead.

Encourage the children to look more closely at individual doors and discuss their colour, shape and the materials they are made of. Is the paint cracked or peeling so that previous paint shows through? Are there any panes of glass? Talk about the shape and position of handles, knobs and letter-boxes. What other added extras such as bells and lamps can the children identify and describe?

Help the children to take photographs and make quick sketches while you are out, so that they have visual reminders of some of the things they noticed.

Follow-up

After your visit, talk with the children about what they saw, using the photographs and drawings as prompts. As they become more confident about discussing doors and door furniture, help them to deduce further information and speculate about possibilities. Ask the children questions such as 'What signs were there that the building was shared by lots of people?' (e.g., several doorbells or name labels on the same door); 'Why was there a handrail on some of the doors?' (aesthetics, the door had steps leading up to it, an elderly person might have lived there); 'Why did some doors have glass in them?' (personal preference or to let light into a dark entrance hall).

Whatever next!

see page 23

This page may be photocopied for use in the classroom and should not be declared in any return in respect of any photocopying licence.

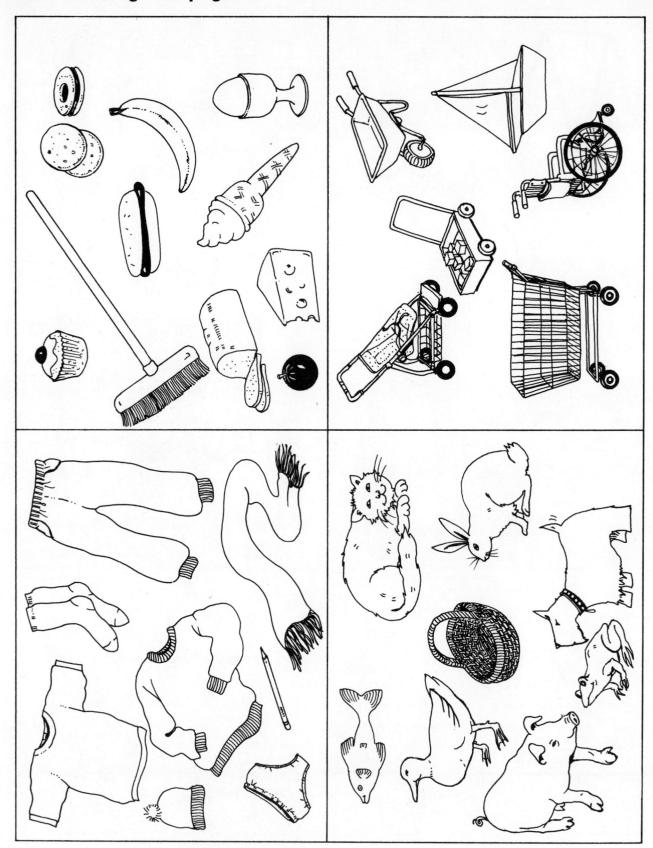

Three bears, three chairs, see page 39

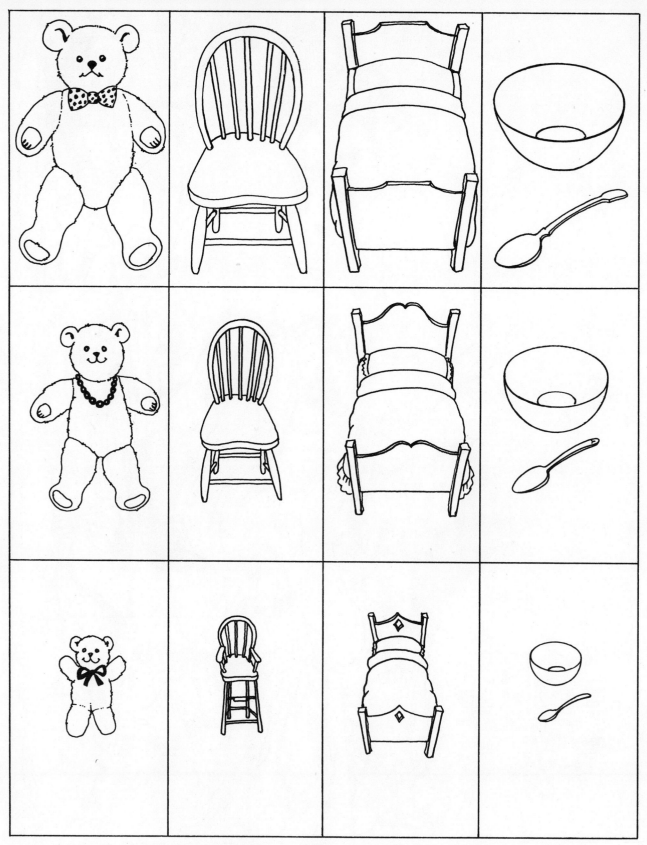

This page may be photocopied for use in the classroom and should not be declared in any return
in respect of any photocopying licence.

Box it up, see page 42

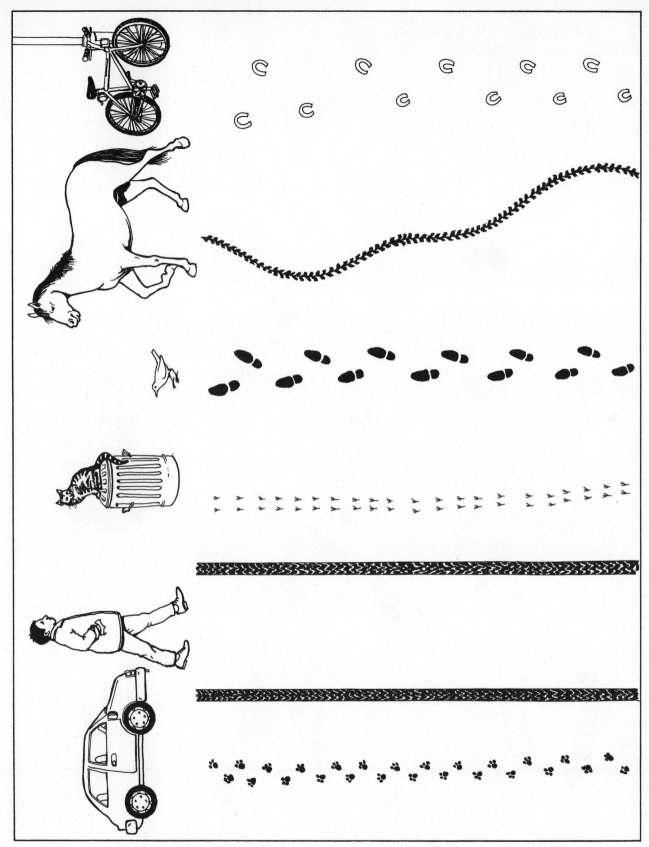

A special present, see page 55

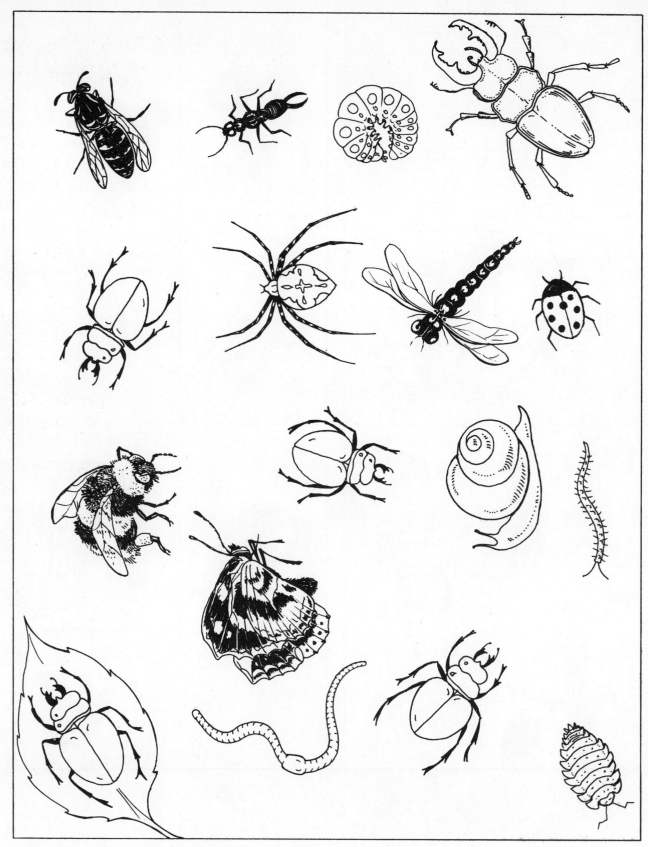